Through the Withering Storm: A Brief History of a Mental Illness

Copyright Leif Gregersen 2009

Foreword by Dr. Brian Bishop

Edited by Raevn Brasch and Nancy Argyle.

Debbie:

Thanks for your support, I hope you have the best summer!

Leif Gregersen

mar. 2013

Through The Withering Storm

Foreword

As a psychiatrist, I am privileged to be given a very personal window into my patients' lives. They trust me and talk about things that they cannot discuss with others. Patients with mental illness, however, are first and foremost, people. Their illnesses may be similar but their personal experiences are all very different. Their experiences are unique because every human brain is unique and it is the brain that determines who we are. Every idea, feeling, decision and action is determined by the delicate machinery that we balance daily on our shoulders without a thought. Mental illnesses happen to people and they don't happen to someone else – they happen to "us." About one in five of us will suffer a mental illness in our lives and so all of us have known somebody with a mental illness, if not ourselves, then someone we work with or meet, on a bus, in a car, in the bank or on the street. Although these illnesses are common, we do not usually talk about them much. No one chooses to be ill and there are no "good" illnesses. They all interfere with our lives. The neurological disorders, particularly the ones we call mental illnesses, are especially disruptive because, when the delicate machinery of our brain goes wrong, so do we.

    Mental illnesses affect individuals, their families, and everyone around them but the costs are not just to lives, careers and families. The social and economic impacts of mental illnesses are slowly being recognized in business, in the armed forces, in our health care system as well as in daily life. Most of these common and very personal situations do not make newspaper headlines. They are private struggles to try to make sense of what may seem an alien, confusing and sometimes hostile world.

Leif has bravely chosen to share his own private struggles during his life and his experience with his own illness. He has given us all the unusual opportunity to share his personal and continuing story.

It is opportune at this time, when some governments see illnesses only in terms of dollars and have forgotten that it is people who get sick, that someone has the courage to make us realize that this is personal. People are hurt by illness and our governments should not be adding to the suffering.

Thank you, Leif, for allowing me the privilege of writing an introduction and for your contribution to the ongoing efforts to remove taboos and ignorance about mental illness.

Dr. Brian Bishop, December, 2009

Through The Withering Storm

Chapter One: The Last Glorious Summer

It was the middle of August 1985 and it was the last of the long and glorious summers I was to have as a kid. For two months, we could laze around, drink tall iced sodas, play with whatever friends we had and generally forget about all the turmoil in the world and the years of work we would have to do before we would finally reach the point where we were finished school and standing tall as fully institutionalized young people.

It still stands out clearly in my mind what those summers meant. They were the icing on a birthday cake, they were the oases in the vast desert of being told where to go, what to do and how hard to climb. From September on, I would often look at the calendar or the slowly ticking clock and count the days, the hours, the minutes, until summer would come

around again. Summer meant trips to the cool and beautiful mountains and the hot and fascinating Badlands of the Drumheller Valley where my favorite uncle lived, and even longer journeys to the interior of British Columbia where the sunshine and the fresh apples made it seem like you were in the Garden of Eden. Those trips meant everything to me. Probably not so much in 1985, but, in earlier years, I can recall that weekends were so precious that I would occasionally be moved to tears on Sunday night knowing I had to go back and face school for five days until another weekend came around. Always in the back of my mind there was the idea that one day when school was over and I could go where I wanted,

I could spend all my time in these beautiful and loving places, far from teachers and bullies and the many things that nearly made life unbearable for me as a child.

It was sad, really because I stuck out in school, having a short haircut when no one else did, and I didn't often care much about my clothes or my general appearance. I liked to read and do well on tests. I didn't like rock and roll music or play sports outside of the pick-up games of football I used to get involved in. Even then though I was always the last picked for the team and had to do twice as good as anyone just to get the ball thrown to me. In short, I was a misfit, a nerd.

Fortunately, a year earlier from this time and place I was in, I found a place where the things I liked mattered, where people approached life a little more seriously, where there was a lot more fun to be had than there ever was at school and I was even able to make a few friends. I found Air Cadets. Joining up was really my mom's idea, although my dad worked with Air Cadets through the local Lions Club. Air Cadets convened every Monday evening (sports night) and Thursday evening (parade night). We often went for weekend camps and there were longer camps called "courses" that many of us would attend in the summer.

Late in the summer of 1985, I was about to attend such a course known only as basic training at a place called Canadian Forces Base Penhold. Penhold was a former Second World War era airmen's training base not far from Red Deer, Alberta, where many courses took place. It remains a cadet training camp to this day, but has been slightly converted so that it is also a jail/boot camp for troubled kids. Sometimes I

Through The Withering Storm

laugh when I think of this place being used for punishment and correction because, back then, everyone I knew was there voluntarily and loved just about every minute of it. There were band camps, flying scholarship camps, junior leaders' camps and of course, basic training. Basic training, for me, would be two weeks of instruction in drill, physical fitness, leadership, survival, and anything else they could cram into two weeks of eight-hour-days for 13-year-olds.

The day I remember most clearly, though, is the one just before camp. I had gotten myself into a bit of trouble with my brother Owen. He was a weight trainer and often liked to lounge around without a shirt on. There was something about this habit of his that irritated me, so, as I was ironing my uniform that day in preparation for camp, I snuck up behind him, and, honestly thinking it would have the same effect of something very cold (making the person jump) I took the very hot iron and touched it to his back. He didn't just jump, he screamed, and then screamed blue bloody murder about what he was going to do to me. I took off like a shot, but he was close behind me, and the only thing that kept me from getting a beating was the fact that I held the iron out in front of myself, promising that it would bite twice if he were to hit me.

I made good my escape as he went to attend to his wound (there is still a mark on his back to this day and he shows it to me often). I decided to avoid him at all costs until I left for camp. By some stroke of luck, I was able to do this, mostly due to my kind sister Kiersten, who, despite her

four-year head start on me, never complained when I wanted to hang out with her and her friends.

6

My brother Owen, on the other hand, used to do things like use code words with his friends when they wanted to ditch me. I would be standing with them and suddenly one of them would yell "three!" or "four!", which was a pre-arranged place to meet and they would run off in different directions leaving me standing there alone and sad that I had no friends or younger brothers.

My sister's friends were cool. There was Shelly, a very sweet and often flirty young woman who had a brother my age and always made me feel special. Then there was Mark Jensen who Kiersten went to church with. On the night before I left for Penhold, I learned that one of my sister's guests had even been to the air base and, then, had been sent home the first day for chatting up a female cadet. He had joined the regular army and was about to leave for more comprehensive basic training. I often wonder where he is now. I never heard from him again, though his stories kept me up half that night.

In those younger days, I was constantly in a state of fantasy, I suppose like most kids, but my fantasies all had to do with armies and war. It came out in the books I read, the movies I watched, and the clothes I wore. It went back a long way, too. I had been an avid collector of GI Joe toys and used to make aircraft models and paint toy soldiers. At that time though, I used to like to volunteer to help with our local Legion because a lot of the older people in the Legion had served in war and I wanted to honor them with my own service.

I managed to get through the night without a beating from Owen and the next morning my dad drove me out to the Canadian Forces Base at Edmonton, where I was to be registered and then sent on to Penhold which was about an hour south on the

Through The Withering Storm

highway from Edmonton. At that age, as with many kids, my dad was my hero. It wasn't a small coincidence that I was named after him as people often found we looked alike and acted alike. My dad was born in Denmark and had been trained extensively to be a sign writer and a businessman, and had served in the Danish military as a fireman and medic, all of which he did exceptionally well. In 1985, times were getting tough, but still he kept food on the table.

Just as my dad was my hero, my mom was my best friend. Genetically, I didn't get the best of the best when I was really thought about my family. My uncle, aunt, grandmother and great-grandmother all suffered from mental illness and nearly all the men on my dad's side were alcoholics. As far as love and devotion went, I couldn't have had better parents. My mom was a highly intelligent person who used to take the time to talk with us for as long as we wanted each and every day, in between her sessions of reading every classic book we had in the house. My dad was so devoted I can remember being read Nobel prize-winning novels as a child of three, and at the same age being taught to play chess and listen to classical music, and although it was often much harsher than I felt it should be, I benefited from my parent's strong discipline and stability in my younger years.

Registering for our camp took several hours and I had time to get to know a few people with whom I was going to take the course. There was one guy who seemed to have only half a vocabulary and the missing half he simply filled in with the word "dink." I was to find out later that he had an aversion to work and, out of probably 300 cadets in basic, he was to end up in my room. There was another fellow who used to walk around wearing a Russian army cap.

He complained to me that some jerk had flushed his stash of illegal drugs down the toilet. Most of the cadets I knew had a low tolerance for that sort of stuff so I wasn't surprised. There were others, but after all these years, the faces and the names have become as indistinguishable as the uniforms. What I do remember is that Air Cadets was the only way out of the small towns and farms for an awful lot of these people. What I also remember about the base in Edmonton was that the food was really bad. The barracks we were in were called the Griesbach (pronounced 'grease-bah'), but most people referred to them as the Grease-Batch barracks. I clearly understood why.

It didn't take me long to find a friend from 533 Squadron back home in St. Albert. His name was Jeff King, he was actually among my very best friends and, before long, I was feeling as much at home on the base as I ever did back in the neighborhood. Soon, we were loaded on buses, driven off to Penhold, where we had our bags searched (I managed to sneak in the most coveted of contraband — pop and chips) and had our rooms assigned. We were formed into flights (or squads) of 30 or so cadets, introduced to the camp's non-commissioned officers (NCOs), who would be our instructors, then issued our camp uniforms and canvas sneakers. After another barely passable meal, we were cut loose.

Having been told to elect a room senior who would be responsible for supervising us in our cleaning and polishing duties, we all chose the same guy. He was the one who had the undeniable leadership quality of being the tallest person in the room. Soon, we were instructed in the methods of cleaning of our rooms which would be inspected daily. Every surface seemed to need a different

Through The Withering Storm

cleaning agent or special cloth. Every bit of dust, every corner of the floor, all the windows, the brass doorknob and window handles had to be polished, shined and cleaned, and done over and over until they were perfect.

I had no problem with these duties but, inside my locked closet (that I was supposed to keep spotless), my personal items were a total mess. Spoiling potato chips, dirty socks, wrinkled clothing. The NCOs couldn't see it so I didn't bother with it and fortunately was never caught. It was an odd thing that when it came down to my image or my reputation as a cadet, I would go the extra mile, dutifully shining boots for an hour each day, pressing my uniform practically whenever I wasn't wearing it, shining everything right down to my belt buckle, but as far as personal hygiene, I slacked off. Rather than wash my hair, I would have the barber cut it as short as he could. Rather than shower each day, I would take a bath about once a week. I didn't realize at the time that this odd behaviour was actually a symptom of an illness. It was something that was sneaking up on me from behind and would soon take me down like a wolf runs down a caribou and goes for the jugular.

The earliest sign I can recall now was that somehow, I was actually a bit scared of being super clean like a lot of the other guys. In a way, my clothes were like a warm and protective womb that I didn't want to leave. I would wear jackets and sweaters even in summer, I was afraid to even unbutton a shirt one button from the top. At camp, I even had pajamas to sleep in and I always wore them, something not one other guy among hundreds did. I now know this is something mentally ill youths do a lot – neglect their cleanliness – but, back then, it just seemed like the natural thing to do. I had no idea that something was boiling up inside of me. Other signs were to follow. The pressure and stress of being a 13 year-old kid far from home surely didn't help.

One of my big problems became apparent once in dealing with the guy in my room who kept saying "dink" whenever his vocabulary failed him. He didn't seem to care much about anything at all. Worse yet, he didn't do the chores that we were assigned as common tasks. At one point, we all got so sick of him that we got a huge cadet whom I only remember by the name of "Acid" to carry him down the hall and dump him in a garbage can. I decided to assist by pushing down his legs as he was struggling to get out and when he did get free he was madder at me than he was at the rest of the guys. This was something that had dogged me for many years It seemed to me at that age that any time I tried to do supposedly 'cool' things, I would be the one singled out to catch all the flak from it. It was so hard for me to make friends with a group and it even seemed like the few friendships I made were with people who only wanted to encourage me to pull one of my stunts. But in this case, I guess this guy figured somehow he could take me in a fight but things never got to that point, at least not from him.

The facilities at camp were pretty good. There was an outdoor pool, a store, a bowling alley, a dance hall, an arcade, and even a library (I may have been the only one in camp to ever use the library). I used the pool a few times but rarely went to actually bowl. For me, the bowling alley served the sole purpose of allowing me to find people I didn't like who were bowling and then reset the pins on them, timing it so that just as their ball was about to hit them, the pins would lift up in the air. Other times, I would watch them hit a few pins and then reset the

Through The Withering Storm

pins so that their small victories could not be recorded. It was cruel but it was the closest thing to good clean fun that could be found. Of course I never would have done this if I wasn't trying to impress my best friend Ian.

The days went by and, soon, I received my first mail from home including some envelopes with a few coins taped together, slipped into the letter. My parents didn't have much money at the time and that was the best they could do. I appreciated the gesture so much that I saved the taped-together coins for years afterwards. I can remember clearly that my sister would even draw her funny cartoons on the tape that held the money together. In my heart of hearts, I missed them all dearly but my hard head wouldn't let on that I was even a little homesick.

My biggest problem at camp was that I used to go around and pick fights with anyone and everyone who thought they were tougher than me, of course with Ian in tow who never fought himself but liked to get me going. One day, I was visiting a friend on the top floor of the barracks and, after an interchange of words, some guy came up and started pushing him. The guy was half my friend's size, but I thought I would show off a bit and kicked him square between the legs with my steel-toed boot. That left him writhing in pain on the ground while I simply walked away.

As I got to the stairs at the other end of the barracks, a cadet came running and said to me, "hey, the captain wants to see you!" I really should have taken off at that point, as it would have made my whole life so much easier, but I went back. This captain was quite upset. He really laid into me but he couldn't stay. He was replaced by a sergeant and the guy I clipped, doubled over in a chair, explaining the story in his words.

"Lurch here came up to me and said I was making friction last night and there were stains on the ceiling so I started pushing him and then this guy came up and kicked me in the balls," he said to the sergeant. It was hard for me not to laugh at this guy's candor. I basically repeated my story, but with a bit of a spin on it. Then a warrant officer came in and asked to hear the story and I added a little more spin, and the chain of command kept going up all the way to major. In the end, I had enough spin on the story so it sounded like I was doing my best to protect my buddy from this wanton masturbator. When it was all sorted out, we were both given the same punishment but I got a mark on my camp record against me. This was yet another case of me not really being in total control of how far I went with things. To think back now I would never dream of kicking someone unless it was a life and limb matter, but to the 'tough guy' thirteen year-old in uniform it just kind of happened.

I loved camp but in a way I could hardly wait for it to end so I could go back to my home town. I felt pretty privileged at times to be receiving all this training and knowledge about guns, planes, first aid and leadership, while most of the people back home were simply trying to decide which soap opera to watch and which one to tape. It was impossible not to swell with pride when I felt the power and esprit de corps of marching in perfect timing with a hundred other people. It made me stronger, mentally and physically, and there was a real sense of direction in my younger life. Aside from standing on top of a mountain in Jasper National Park, which I did later on, it was about the best feeling I had ever

Through The Withering Storm

experienced, maybe because I was starting to grow into being my own person. Here, I didn't have to be afraid to stand tall like I did in school, where you never really knew if a friend would betray you or not for whatever fad came along. Basically we were all the same. A huge unit all working towards one goal, bettering ourselves so we could go home at the end of summer and give something back to our home squadrons.

The last few days of camp went by quickly. As hot August days began to turn into cool, breezy, rainy fall evenings, I knew this couldn't go on forever. This was the end of the summer and I had only been there two weeks. Some of the cadets on course had been there six weeks and some of the staff was there longer. I couldn't understand why some of the other cadets I ran into were literally crying at the idea of camp being over.

Outwardly, I was glad to know that I could sleep in for a few days before school started and that I would be back to the comforts of home. What I didn't realize is that some of these six-week cadets had made close friends and probably even closer girlfriends that summer and would most likely never see them again. I had some really screwed up priorities.

When the last day of basic training came, I had achieved the honor of having the highest mark on the final exam in my flight – a perfect score of 100 per cent. That gave me a bit of leverage when I had to go back home to 533 Squadron and explain why I had been disciplined for attempting to sterilize someone without surgical instruments.

When I got home to my parent's house, I can still remember the song that defined the times for us back then. My sister played it often, and it could be found blasting out of the radio practically wherever there was one. It was Bruce Springsteen's *Born in the USA*. I had heard it many times before someone explained to me that it wasn't any kind of patriotic anthem, it was a song that spoke out against injustices like the Vietnam War and the wars that were to come. It was a song that protested the almighty dollar shitting all over people whom only want to live, love and have children.

In cadets, I was influenced a lot by people who were very conservative, believing that a person had to pull their own weight and, if they didn't, they were of no use to society. Then there were people my sister knew who were very much more leftist and believed in the equality of all mankind. Inside my own head, there was a battle between those two ideologies and a battle for me just to keep my sanity in a society where the only place I felt like I belonged (my home town) was a place where a lot seemed to go against my values, as they were forming.

My heroes at that time were people like Gandhi who changed the world by making his enemies look into their own souls. At the time though, I was a part of the defense structure and it was difficult for me to reconcile that with the peaceful side of me. I guess that's why they called us Generation X when I got older. Not a lot made sense to me, especially that it didn't seem fair that we were cold warriors in a time when warriors were no longer heroes.

These philosophical questions and all the pressures of being a teenager were starting to get to me. I may have gotten perfect marks on my cadet evaluation but somehow I wasn't firing on all cylinders. Coming home from basic training was going to be one of the last times in my life that I had a clear idea of what I wanted and what the world

Through The Withering Storm

wanted from me. It was the beginning of a horrific ride down a long and slippery slope.

Not long after basic training, I began grade nine – the final year of junior high and the final step before the long-awaited (and feared) start of high school. Being in the last grade of junior high was a huge rite of passage for most of us. It was sort of the defining line between being a child and being a young adult. Not to mention that next year we would mainly be going to school with academic students — a lot of the others would go to trade or vocational schools. I still remember my sister's grade nine graduation, how she got all fancied up in a pretty dress, had a date in a white tux, and how happy she seemed.

But, by now, my sister had reached the golden age of 18 and moved out and I had my own room. It didn't bother me that it was painted in girl colors, it only mattered that it was my space to organize my growing collection of military clothing and collection of war books. I had a place to hide my air rifles from my parents and somewhere that I could listen to rock music, which I was now finally beginning to like. Soon, I would be changing from black to white in many ways.

In every grade of every school like mine, there is one knock-out girl and Sir George Simpson Junior High was no exception. Her name was Mandy, she was amazing and, by some stroke of luck, she was in my class. I think she knew she was exceptionally good looking because she always used to come into class fashionably late so she could put on a show of prancing through the class in the always-new clothes her wealthy father had provided. Not only was Mandy gorgeous, she was incredibly smart and would often get 100 per cent on tests – the same tests that no one else in the class did well.

Being a former 'nerd' or 'brain' and a highly competitive person, this really irked me. I even had a theory about why she was so rich, smart and attractive. It was simply because of Darwinian genetics. This girl was the result of thousands of years of evolution. The pretty and smart ones always get a mate and pass down their attractiveness and intelligence until you breed someone special like Mandy. It killed me thinking of how I was short-changed but, still, secretly, I could hardly take my eyes off her.

I had a lot of respect for the people in cadets and took it very seriously but had very little respect for school and teachers along with a lot of the people with whom I went to school. One the big reasons for this attitude was that our math and science teacher that year had an obvious drinking problem and it really made me feel ripped off to constantly have substitute teachers. I was getting a second class education because some guy couldn't handle his alcohol. I was starting to feel a lot of animosity towards 'drunks' as I called them and I took a lot of that animosity out on the subs. The sad thing was that I wasn't just lashing out because of my teacher; my dad was quite far into a problem of his own. I still got pretty good grades but fooled around a lot. It wasn't unusual to see me wrestling teachers, blowing up electrical sockets, stealing future tests to pass out to the class, and signing out library books with embarrassing titles for other people. Like the time I signed a bunch of books about puberty which the teacher read the list out loud in front of the class, causing my poor victim to nearly throw a fit.

Though I was close to six foot tall at age 14, I wasn't the biggest or strongest kid in school. A jerk named Donald was and he was also in my class. He constantly picked on me. If we were playing hockey in gym, he would bash me from behind. If I was leaning back in my chair, he would try and tip it over. There are times I wanted to literally kill him. When you added that to the fact I was getting into increasingly loud and violent fights with my dad, you are left with a "me" that was under a lot of pressure both at home and in school. I sometimes wonder why I never tried to kill myself back then.

In my seat in the back of the room, I was also not far from a girl named Laurie, who had failed grade nine and was now in her second year of it. I really don't know why, but at one point in that school year, she joined Air Cadets and became good friends with most of my own friends in cadets. She never made much indication of liking me, though we would often talk about our friends and parties we went to. While a lot of people in grade nine were having pop and chip parties, people in cadets were flying down the highway in brand new $30,000 trucks shooting real pistols at road signs, going on trips all over the place, flying gliders and small planes, and being taught how to teach others and lead them. And cadets were often going to parties or dances and drinking the hard stuff.

This made a lot of people in the ninth grade jealous and some of them actually wanted to try and join up but I warned them all that if they wanted to join they would be my subordinates and I wouldn't treat them all that well. I guess people's image of me was evidence enough that they did not want to become my subordinate because none of them tried to join. I haven't spoken to Laurie in years but I think it is possible she took on a military career after we completed grade 12. The military became so much a part of us that when we quit or got too old for cadets, it was the next natural step to join the regular forces.

The days and weeks and months rolled by and I spent a lot of time at cadet weekend camps and with my friends in cadets – among them , Frank, Jim and Kyle (who hated his first name much so we all called him Lurch all the time). He was my best friend for a long time after that, and I still talk to Frank quite a bit to this day. There were bush camps, band camps, leadership camps and Sunday range night with real Second World War rifles converted to .22 caliber. Cadets provided an extremely full life for a kid who didn't have much. Lurch and I used to put our whole lives into being the best cadets we could be. Lurch was in the colour party, the group that carried our flags for parades, and I was in the band, marking the cadence for the whole squadron with my snare drum. Even though we lived about three miles apart and went to school in different cities, he and I would get together nearly every day. When weekend camps came around, we would train like athletes to be in shape for them. We would go totally gung-ho when we were there. I remember now there were small signs to me (perhaps larger ones to my parents) that I was getting worse mentally. Of course, my clothes were a red flag because they were nearly always army fatigues. Then, there was the fascination I had with fire, knives and my fear of social situations like dating and dancing.

During that time, one of the worst symptoms was one that no one could see. I kept thinking that I could hear my name being called, even in an empty house. This would go on for a few hours, especially after a major cadet event, and then it would just go away. Somehow, through sheer will, I would keep sitting still through a phase of mania. By doing this, I would not respond to this delusion but it was getting harder and harder to do.

My other good friend, Frank, gave me a book called *Truly Tasteless Jokes* for my birthday that year. It was divided into sections, from Polish to Black to Jewish and so on. I read that book through a dozen times thinking it would make me popular but in fact it ended up disgusting a lot of girls in whom I had an interest. I was the clown to all my friends that year. Clearly, there were no more boundaries for me, and whatever dark forces that hid inside my mind were taking what the world was throwing at me and turning me into just about the exact opposite of a normal kid my age.

Jim, another friend, who was Frank's best friend, seemed like a bit of a stoner back then, but really was quite a thoughtful and intelligent guy and a pretty good athlete (just like Frank in those respects I suppose, but I don't think Frank ever did drugs). Jim always seemed to be getting into trouble but put a lot into cadets. He also swam, skied and went for long-distance cycle trips all the time. I hate to say it, but I think when I was eventually promoted to corporal, the three of them got frustrated because of not getting promoted themselves and none of them followed through into a third year of cadets with me. I made new friends who I thought were good people but they ended up to be far worse jerks than I think I ever associated with in my life.

In school, I had this one teacher who was actually really nice but a bit heavy. One time, I was in the library after school while he was there, and I said, "Hey, Mr. Wiselin! I saw a book here about you!"

He seemed so happy and said, "Oh, really? What book is that, Leif?" So, I showed him the book,

with the title 'Ancient Greece' and he went nuts,
throwing me into an arm hold and slammed me into a
wall. All I could do was laugh, because I had gotten
to him. I used to consider it a personal challenge
whenever we had a new teacher or a substitute to see
if I could break them. I kept all the people in my class
in stitches, but none of it was respect, none of it was
caring.

Mr. Wiselin gave us a lot of lectures that
year, and one day I started to notice that he would
walk to one place, sit down for a while, then go to the
edge of his desk, sit down for a while, and so on.
These little resting spots soon became predictable, so I
noted them and one day put a tack on each one. Not
one tack on his chair, five or six tacks on each spot he
favored. Sadly though, none of them hit home, or so I
thought. The whole class had seen me put the tacks in
the spots though, and it was absolutely gut-splitting to
have 30 young people sit breathless as poor Mr.
Wiselin sat down on each of his favorite spots.

No yelps or painful outcries took place
though, but one girl told me later that she nearly peed
herself laughing seeing him walk down the hall with a
tack stuck in his jeans that had somehow missed all of
his nerves.

Along with the cadet camps, there were also
cadet dances and, of course, cadet parties. I went to
probably every dance, almost always wore a military
combat uniform and would sit down, talk with my
friends, drink a pop and then leave when the dance
was over. My appreciation of rock music was quite
new, though our DJ, who was also a drummer in our
cadet band, my snare drum instructor, could really put
on a show for us. I had a terrible shyness and was
very worried about looking silly on the dance floor, so
I was just a spectator all the time, but it was an Air

Through The Withering Storm

Cadet function so I always went. One time, a senior cadet on whom I had a crush, literally begged me to dance. It was a slow dance and she had a really nice body but I kept refusing until she quit trying. It was such a shame. I think she knew I liked her and took it as a compliment, but I was totally locked inside myself. That was the worst part of life I had to go through, the feeling that I didn't deserve to be loved. I knew my family loved me but that meant very little to me because they had to love me and I really thought to myself that any grown person who relies on his family to feel loved was a loser.

One time, I was at a dance close to Christmas and some friends and I decided to go to the corner store, after which we were walking around. A car drove past us and the people in it yelled at us and I yelled back "f**k you!" in an extremely loud voice. The car pulled up to us and stopped and I apologized and told them I thought they were some people we knew. They drove off and we walked on. A few minutes later, they turned around, parked their car, got out of it, and started walking towards us. I figured everything was cool, so when one guy came up to me, I said, "Man, I'm sorry about what I said. For a minute I thought you were going to kick the shit out of us."

"You mean like this," he replied and suddenly a foot came out of nowhere and smashed into the side of my face. I had never seen anyone kick like that and didn't know what to do, so I took off running and he kept coming after me. Before I could get to the safety of a nearby store, he was on top of me. I curled up into a ball and he started to kick me as hard as he could. Some guy in a nearby truck got out and stopped him. After finding out that I was okay, he had the kindness to give me a ride home.

It was weird the way those kinds of events would effect me. I could stand up, take the blows, give a few, but when I got home and was alone, it would eat my insides up worrying about why people hated me so much and why these things kept happening to me. When I got in the door, with a puffed up face and a shiner coming through, I was overcome with the sadness of my separation from the rest of the world, proved through this random beating. When my parents looked at me I started to cry. That was the worst night of my young life.

At one dance, Frank invited us to go outside with him because he needed a smoke and we complied, being a tightly knit group. He lit up and passed his cigarette over to me. I took one puff and nearly coughed my lungs up. All my friends had a good laugh over that and I swore that wouldn't humiliate me again so I "practiced" smoking out my window each night with one cigarette before bed. Soon, I was using every kind of tobacco, pipe, cigars, cigarettes and even the odd chew. Within two years, I was up to two packs a day and had dropped out of every physical activity I had ever been involved in. Smoking took a real toll on me and it took 18 years for me to quit. Since then, I learned that smoking actually releases a chemical in a person's brain similar to some psychiatric drugs. Apparently, it is no small coincidence that 50 per cent of all cigarettes sold are sold to mentally ill people who represent only between 5-20 per cent of the general population.

There was another incident in grade nine that made me feel like bad things happened to me for some twisted divine purpose. As I mentioned, I didn't get along with too many of the groups that were established in school. A student named Stuart, who was a hockey player, liked to pick on me a lot. He would do stupid things, like walk up and shove me for no reason or make fun of my name. One time, he phoned me up and asked if I wanted to fight him. My dad was on the other phone listening in when this happened but nothing came of it. Then, one day things boiled up. I was walking down the hall and he pushed me. I pushed back and said "F**k you, Stuart!"

"F**k you, Leif!" he replied. "Wanna fight?"

"Sure," I said, "Any time." Cadets were probably not the best at sports but we fought like the dickens all the time. I had nothing to worry about from this guy. A time and place was established and, when I showed up, practically the whole school was there. Stuart and I squared off and I used my favorite tactic of simply throwing myself into the fight and letting my superior wrestling skills win out. This time was no exception and after a few minutes of struggling, I put my opponent into a throw that took him right down. Then, I got on top of him and held him so there was no way for him to move. From there, I didn't know what to do. I rarely ever punched in a fight and, in just about every tussle I had been in, it was all about who was the better fighter, not who could inflict the most damage. He squirmed and struggled, but there was no way he was getting up.

"It's over Stuart!" I said.

"I'm gonna f**king kill you!" he said to me.

"Let's split them up and start the whole thing over again!" some bitchy sounding young female said. I could feel people spitting on me from the crowd and I knew these people had come to see blood, not a fair fight. So, I just got up. I stood right up, let Stuart go and walked off. He came after me and threw a whole lot of punches at my face but, in fact, they didn't hurt much. He had probably never been in a fight outside of a peewee hockey game. The funny thing is that I never held a grudge about those punches to the face. I did hold a grudge against was the a**hole Donald, who came up and joined in the fracas by throwing me over a fence so I landed on my back. That act made me so bloody angry (and still does) that I don't know what I would do if I ever found that guy again.

Again, when I got home, I couldn't understand why people were like this, why they were bloodthirsty, backstabbing and hateful. I swore that would be my last fight ever, at least my last schoolyard fight. I wouldn't be a performing monkey for these people who had no respect for me, my family or the things for which I stood. I would have kept my word too, but one day not all that many years in the future, a frightening blood lust rose in me that I was unable to control.

One of the few respites I had from the pressures of school and home was shooting. I had two air rifles and used to pretend I was a sniper by hanging out my window, shooting at leaves for target practice. Sometimes, I would shoot my neighbour's windows, then hide in my room and hear them come out and search around to no avail for what had made the loud sound. I honestly thought all that was happening was a loud sound, until one day I had a friend over and my parents were out and an RCMP officer came knocking at my door.

Apparently, I was actually shooting holes in the windows and causing quite a bit of damage. I really felt bad about it, I even promised all of my summer camp salary to go towards the damages. Little did I know that $120 salary I would have coming for the camp I had chosen would have been a drop in a bucket. To this day, I wonder why I never had to go to court for that. My dad told me recently that I had caused about $6,000 worth of damage in the shootings. On the other hand, my brother had been caught shoplifting a cassette tape and he was charged, had to go to court and was sentenced to a year's probation, but for some reason I didn't even have to pay for the broken windows. Our neighbour's house insurance covered the bill. I often wonder what would have happened with my life if I had been charged and sent to a reform school. God must have intervened on my behalf back then.

My main motivation for the shooting was that I had a strong disliking for a girl my age that lived in that house, chiefly because when her family moved in, a good friend of my brother and mine moved out. So, in a dumb kid's way, we blamed her. Ironically, I am now friendly with that girl and we play long-distance word games on the Internet. She even married a soldier.

It was interesting the way my parents dealt with me getting caught with air rifles they had no knowledge of – especially considering that my dad had been a conscientious objector when he did his service time in Denmark and he had elected to become a member of the fire brigade rather than carry a gun. He had seen horrors during the war he often related to me when he was past all comprehension drunk. If it weren't for the stories he told me late at night, I would never have loved him as much as I did and I probably would have run away. I'm sure also a part of him must have hated me for being a combat-uniform-wearing, gung-ho air cadet. In dealing with my shooting incident though, my parents simply had a talk with me and allowed me to set up my own pellet gun range in the basement. This made me truly happy because I could now sit for hours drinking tea and setting up targets or old toy soldiers, picking them off one by one. I could also invite Lurch over to sit down there and talk for hours. Sometimes we would stay up and play video games, drink coffee and tea and talk until the sun came up. It became a tradition with us, one we carried on through a number of years and good and bad times.

    As the year wore on, I was having increasing difficulties at school, with my grades and my attitude and, at home, with the terrible fights with my dad. After a while, I left my parents no choice. They sent me to see a psychiatrist and the meeting didn't go well. That day is still clear to me. I wore a dark green Canadian Forces uniform, my short hair wasn't combed or washed, and I sat nervously answering questions from a man I had never met before and in whom I had little confidence. The end result of that short and sweet interview was that he wanted me to come into a psychiatric ward for a week for observation. I was devastated. It didn't make any sense to me. I couldn't see myself from the outside and I had no friends to bounce my mental deficiencies off. As far as I was concerned, I wasn't suffering from the same illness I had watched my mom go through these past many years and numerous hospitalizations. I was a victim of the violence that was the result of my dad's drinking and the bullying I had endured through most of my school years to that point. It was an incredibly egotistical and selfish belief I had, but I actually believed my dad hated me because I was smarter and more successful than him. My dad often used to say he had half of a grade 12 education, he had grade six.

    I didn't think this was a fair qualification to manage the life of a young Einstein like myself. Hadn't I figured out on a computer how to calculate a mortgage when most kids weren't sure what a mortgage was? Hadn't I earned honors in grade eight and accolades in basic training? Little did I realize that my dad was probably twice the genius I was for fighting his way up and out of a war-torn country to fly halfway around the world and build a successful corporation in a place where he didn't even know the language. In my current state of thinking, it didn't seem right.

I did go to the hospital and I spent that week in almost total rebellion. It wasn't a nice place to be but, when I look back, it wasn't anywhere near as bad as places I would one day go. I had my own room and there was a pool table there. No one forced me to go to school or do anything really. I think the one thing that bothered me the most was that I couldn't smoke and there really was no place for me to exercise. It was also a place that exposed me to so many sick people – something that, in my middle-class world, I hadn't realized even existed. I had a lot of misconceptions about psychiatric wards, first of all that being around these people could make me 'crazy'.

I remember being scared when a guy came up to me and told me nicely where the TV was and then I saw a huge river of spittle come rolling out his mouth. It was terrifying because I didn't think I could avoid becoming such a person if I were kept there.

My object became to do everything I could to thwart anyone from helping me, getting close to me or putting me down as anything but an abused but normal kid. I knew that the nurses would make their rounds about every half hour so I would pretend to be asleep when they came. When they left, I would take out a book I had brought about the war in the desert during the Second World War and read it for a few minutes, then go back to pretending to be asleep in time for the next round. Every now and then, I would sneak out of my room and take handfuls of crackers and jam from the snack area with the intention of using them for my many hikes with friends into the wilderness around my hometown.

Every time I was interviewed or asked why I thought I was there, I said pretty much the same thing. My dad is an alcoholic and we fight all the time and because of this I act up sometimes and it's his fault I am here. That is what I believed. I had no concept there was anything wrong with me, even though I must admit, the red flags had been flying for quite some time.

At the end of the week, my family came and I thought my mom was going to back me up, explain to them that my dad was fighting with me and hitting me. That was what she told me when I told her I didn't want to go into the institution. She said it might help my dad to get some counseling.

When the doctor started asking questions about what the problem was, I was stunned when my mom said, "No, it's you." I felt so totally betrayed by the one person in the world I thought actually cared about me. I literally came out swinging, with tears running down my face. My brother started hitting me and my dad started hitting me and I started hitting back. When the smoke cleared, the doctor said he was going to keep me there for another week. I cried and cried that night. I didn't know who I was or what I had done wrong. I thought people were supposed to be proud of their soldiers. Everything, I did stemmed from a desire to, one day, become a soldier and to be the best one I could possibly be.

Surprisingly, while I was incarcerated, I was allowed to attend parade night at cadets and I was promoted to the rank of corporal. It all seemed so meaningless to me – the idea that I was being rewarded, on one hand, for behavior that I was incarcerated for on the other. I felt like a complete piece of garbage, having to return to the psychiatric ward after cadets.

It was that night that I discovered something about myself. The more I isolated myself the worse my social skills became. It was scary because this was one of the first times that I could have believed that I had an illness. Each cadet in 533 squadron was required to either teach a class or take a class and, at that time, I was taking a course on public speaking taught us by a former squadron member who was in Toastmasters. It was really a wonderful course but that night, after having spent seven days hiding in my room in the hospital, I was called on to speak about my hobby of collecting genuine military uniforms. I was a wreck. I was shaking badly, I was a deep shade of red, and, for whatever reason, I was so self conscious and nervous that I couldn't keep eye contact, something in me literally pulled my head down like I was experiencing 3g's of force.

The only thing I can compare to that horror was being injected with a major tranquilizer that took over all of your muscles to the point where you literally bend over backward. Many times, I wished I was a doctor so that I could find that chemical in a person's makeup and work my whole life to eliminate it from the human race. But in reality I am just a sufferer and a client. I will never forget those cutting words I heard of one of the people who was in my class, mocking my 'speech of fear' to a young woman we both knew.

When I got back to the hospital from receiving my promotion, I sat in my room at a reading table hunched over, holding my coveted corporal's stripes, sobbing with the pain I felt and the utter loneliness and rejection. I felt right on the edge of self-destruction and uselessness that night. It was the worst feeling I had ever experienced.

I don't know exactly when I made the decision but, soon after that night, I decided I was going to run away. Not just from the hospital, but from school, my family, from everything. I had a pretty good plan going for me. My sister was coming to take me out on a day pass and I told her they said I could stay out overnight.

I would simply pack a bag that had more than I needed for just an overnight stay and leave it by the door of her apartment. Then, I would grab it and say I was going to the 7-Eleven or whatever and head for the wilderness, in which I was more than experienced at surviving. There was little that could stop me and, if I made it to the forests, there was probably no one who could find me.

My sister came and got me and as we were walking out, she smiled at the nurse and said, "He's going to stay with his sister tonight!"

"Oh, f**k!" I thought. Escape was meters away and she has messed up the whole plan.

"No, wait a minute, he's only allowed to be out for a few hours," the nurse said. One little sentence, a few little words changed my whole life. I could have made it on my own. I was a smart kid and I was convinced I could have lasted for months. But, instead, I was trapped inside a freaking mental ward at age 14.

I know now that running away was no solution but I don't know if sending me back to my parents was any solution either. Something would have to give eventually and it turned out, a few years later, that it was me.

Through The Withering Storm

When I left the hospital, the doctor prescribed me some pills that I took for a while, but I couldn't stand the odd feeling of being light headed all the time. I was against drugs of all kinds back then, and my doctor had never explained that I had an illness or what illness he thought I had that would require this medication. The pills were promptly flushed down the toilet. It was an easy thing to do because no one really seemed to care. I think it was about five months later when my dad noticed that he hadn't replenished the pills for me. I told him what I had done with them and that I felt I was comparatively fine. He was mad, but in his belief, it was my life when it came right down to it. I'd bought myself some fashionable clothes and had started to turn away slightly from the extreme behavior. Little did I know that I was only repressing it. I remember arguing with him, saying that the doctor told me I had too many ups and downs and the pills would stabilize them (though at no time did he use the words bipolar or manic-depressive) and I felt that if you take away ups and downs you are just a zombie that doesn't feel anything.

At that time, I was addicted to a drug of sorts; I was a total adrenalin junkie. Having my own room was great because I was a good climber and my room had a window that opened to the front of the house which had sort of a shelf I could lower myself onto and sneak out at night and climb back in without using a door. Most of the time, I would instead wait for my dad to go to bed, then go in the bathroom, count off a few seconds, then flush the toilet and use the noise of the flush to sneak downstairs. Then, I would stay up often all night watching old black and white shows, drinking tea, making microwave hot dogs and doing a workout I found in a Ninja book. Other times, I would actually sneak out to meet up with friends, or just wander the neighborhood. Luckily, I didn't fall into the criminal element in St. Albert or start going out at night to steal things. In a way, I was still being influenced by the comic books I had read as a kid, especially Batman, who was totally dedicated to doing what was right. I felt like going on my adventures at night was more like training. I saw doing things like climbing the school or wandering the streets as a challenge, not an extra source of income. When people I thought were my friends were doing this sort of thing, breaking into cars or stealing musical instruments from the school to pawn them, I was appalled. Not least of all because they were from considerably more well-off families than mine.

    A big reason for the changes in behavior and clothing was that I had finally really started to take an interest in girls, though the only real knowledge I had of them was what I got out of Playboys my dad left sitting around or late night soft-porn movies and a few of the disgusting jokes I'd read. I had no concept of love or devotion or romance or any of that. Women meant sex and sex was supposed to be the end-all, be-all of life for men. It was a powerful enough force to turn me from a combat-clothing-wearing teenybopper to a well-dressed young man.

    It was around this time, as I neared the end of grade nine, that I started to be influenced by my sister and her boyfriend, a communist immigrant from Greece, who had grand plans of changing the world by getting a political science degree. They kept talking about how there would be blood in the streets in 10 years and how messed up our society was. It took a long time but, after a while, I became infected by their rhetoric and started to look negatively at

Through The Withering Storm

everything including my friends, the air cadet movement, having a job, owning things and so on.

When I first met this guy I was almost going to report him to the authorities as a communist spy. I told my sister about this and she flipped. "Do you realize he could be deported!" she said. I kind of liked that idea but I didn't report him – probably only because I didn't know where to.

This guy was a real slob. I remember going over to their apartment frequently and there was no furniture but a kitchen table. He would be sitting there in his underwear, (if he wore that much clothing for company) eating with all the noise one person could muster, insulting me for wearing a tie. I used to tell him how repulsive his eating was and he would say that where he worked (for a forestry company) food to them was just fuel and it didn't matter how it was consumed. It made me sick to my stomach, and, possibly because of the big impression he had on my sister, it made me begin to doubt my very image of myself.

That was pretty much the end of air cadets for me. Though I stayed on for one more year, my heart and soul just wasn't in it. Close to the end of my grade nine year, when we were going through the process of applying for our summer camps, on a Monday sports night I sustained a serious injury. We were playing a game called 'stick in the middle.' We were split into two teams and numbered off, with the same numbers on opposing sides of the gym (one to 10) and a hockey stick was placed in the middle of the two groups. Without warning, the leader of the game would call out a number and the two people who were assigned that number would have to run full tilt and literally fight for the stick, and then bring it back to their side.

This time, luck was not with me and a cadet named Todd Reader, two years my senior, had my number. I didn't back down though. I went towards the stick full on and somehow my foot got twisted around under Todd and he got the stick and got it away from me, leaving me writhing in pain on the floor. I limped off to the sidelines and one of the senior cadets, a young woman (who I had a complete crush on) asked to see my foot. I told her I was okay and since sports night was nearly over, I figured I just had a sprain and could go home and rest my foot and it would be fine in the morning. When I got home (after the ritual hamburger we gorged on after every cadet night), my foot was in even more pain. I ended up getting my dad to drive me to the hospital where I found out it was broken.

This didn't sit well with me because we had to take a medical to complete the application process for our camps, and when it came time to answer the question of whether or not I would be okay to march on a hard surface, the doctor ticked 'no' and I failed the medical. I had it re-done, but, by the time I resubmitted my application, the junior leadership course I really wanted was filled, and I ended up getting the air crew survival course, where they sent all the slackers. It was a two-week course at the same camp where our squadron went for weekends during the year. Still, I guess I was lucky, because only half of the guys who applied for courses got one and I liked the idea of training in the bush. I was going to have some fun, despite myself.

It was so hard for me to accept that I had limits, that my bones could be broken. The weekend after I broke my foot, we had a camp and because of my injury I couldn't go. I think it was the first such event I had ever missed. These bush camps

Through The Withering Storm

where everyone wore their army clothes and worked on survival and combat skills were my favorite part of cadets. I had so much fun going to them that often I would go without sleep for the whole weekend. On that Saturday night, I went downstairs after my parents were asleep and I soaked my cast in hot water and took a pair of scissors and cut it off. My dad woke up and saw me sitting there with all that plaster splashed in the dining room and promptly took me to the hospital. The next cast they put on broke because I wouldn't stop walking on it (in those days I would walk a mile every day to get cigars). My doctor decided to make a deal with me. He would take the cast off and not put another one on provided I took it easy on the foot. I was such a jerk back then I wouldn't let anyone sign my cast. I don't know if I hated myself or if it was the illness. I just couldn't let myself be human. Humans were weak, friends were disposable, and family was to be controlled. I hate to say it but when I look back through the eyes I have now, I was a monster. At least, part of me was. Part of me wanted love and happiness. Part of me wanted to self-destruct.

After that the bush camp was over, there wasn't much time left in the school year for anything but our grade nine graduation ceremony and there wasn't much to that. In fact, when I heard it was on the same night as my favorite TV show, I nearly backed out of it. Had it been on a cadet night, I never would have gone. It was held in the school gym, it wasn't mandatory to wear a tux and there would be a few parties afterwards.

I was lucky because, although I was only 14, I fit my dad's clothes, so I wore his dark blue three-piece suit to the ceremony. I was bit proud that I actually did make it because, even though I worked hard in some parts, and there were more than a couple of As on my report card, I had nearly been kicked out of school a few times, and for the last third of the school year I did very little work. My Grade 9 diploma had a space waiting for it next to my basic training diploma and that was that. I had thought to myself when I saw those two together that smaller men had built empires on less.

The really big thing I remember about that night was how great Mandy looked. She had on a grad dress that was probably more expensive than most dresses girls buy for their high school graduation, she had a fabulous tan and a 1980s big hairstyle that was just killer. At one point, she was walking through the schoolyard with a friend and I was walking down an adjacent street in my dad's suit and she said to me, "So, Leif, I guess in 10 years we will be seeing you on the stock market." That really blew me away. They were probably the last kind words any attractive female said to me for at least the next six years. I would never forget that night and I will never forget how good she looked. Often, I wish I could forget about Mandy but likely because she was a 'first crush', I probably won't. As years have gone past, I often wonder having heard a thing or two about her whether she was just very nice or just very much a tease and a user. I doubt I will ever know.

Summer started soon after that and it was to prove to be one of my better ones. Despite the fact that I had been 'marked' by the doctor on the psychiatric ward and betrayed by my family, I was still young enough to believe somewhat in who I was and what I was doing. That was a lot more than I would be able to say for a number of years after that.

Chapter Two: Losing Myself, Piece by Piece

The summer of 1986 was another memorable one. At the age of 14, I had taken up the habit of smoking cigars and walking around in dress pants, shirt and tie. I even wore this get-up to one of my first job interviews, to become an ice-cream cart operator. The man who was to be my boss had on some dirty jeans and a t-shirt and was out of cigarettes, so I offered him a cigar. I must have been quite a sight. I did get the job and it wasn't so bad. I remember being out one day for the whole day after classes had ended and being hungry the whole time. Because my school was always within 100 meters of the house I grew up in, making my own lunch was not on my roster of skills. What I did was open a can of ham and simply started making sandwiches. I didn't want to leave anything to go bad so I ended up making about 10 sandwiches, which took a whole loaf of bread. I was well fed that day. Near to vomiting but well fed.

One of the first things I did was help get Lurch a job at the ice cream company. He did his tasks by the numbers, in grand military fashion, and by his third day had his cart running better and colder than any of the others. Lurch was what most people would call hard core, perhaps even more so than me. For starters, at 14 he was 6'3" and stronger and meaner than most grown men. He had total dedication and a solid work ethic like no one I knew. People often thought of him as my bodyguard but, as far as ability went, few were as evenly matched as Lurch and I. I know this because as best friends we competed at everything from video games to wrestling and weight lifting and marksmanship.

The weirdest thing was that it seemed that Lurch and I complemented each other really well. His dad was a mechanic and he knew every home repair or fixit trick from waterproofing shoes to changing and repairing a tire. My skills were more academic and I had a warehouse of theoretical knowledge that matched with his practical knowledge. Like me, though, he was a little crazy. I used to feel bad for him because his parents were strict Mormons and they didn't really know how to deal with a problem child. Neither did my parents but he had eight siblings to compete with, and often his parents would go through his stuff and find things like a book I had given him or a knife he had got at camp and punish him severely for it. He often used to say that his parents were communists, though they were probably closer to the other end of the spectrum. Once he told me that his parents had started taking him to psychiatrists when he was three years old, and this bothered him greatly. And, like me, cadets was the only place where he wanted to succeed, to do well, to learn something.

Lurch got the job easy enough, and worked hard at it, but neither of us made much money mainly because our boss was ripping us off. He would give us eight boxes of popsicles or ice cream cones and then put down that we had taken 10. We could sell 100 ice creams, which was supposed to make us $12.00 and when we got back our slim profits would go to our employer's drug habits. Hard to believe a guy could make his living stealing from kids who were too young to even get a regular job, but he did.

Canada Day that year was a heck of a day for me. Despite the fact my profit was only about 12 cents a cone, I ended up making about $50, which eventually went to supplying my growing cigar habit and my odd addiction to military clothing which went

Through The Withering Storm

against the grain of all fashion at the time. I was a welcome customer at the surplus stores in Edmonton, even selling my old comic books at one store in St. Albert, hoping to make enough to go into Edmonton to buy items such as utility belts or insignia for my uniforms. At the height of my collecting, my closet must have contained eight or nine complete uniforms, worth hundreds of dollars. If I had half that value put into normal kids' clothing I probably would have been the best dressed kid in town.

It wasn't long into the summer of '86 that I had to leave for my course, the same one that my brother had taken two years earlier, called air crew survival. My brother, Owen, did have good marks in classes the cadets taught, and could shoot pretty well. He was even in the color party and carried the Canadian flag on parade nights. But he was constantly getting into trouble for his long hair, his earring and various other unforgivable offences. From what he told me, and what I heard from my friends, air crew training was no picnic. It consisted of eight days of intensive, hands-on survival training and then a final exam that took place in the woods with nothing but bare minimum equipment and one meal. You had to survive like that for five days. It seemed impossible. I remember asking how many kids had died on the course. Fortunately, none had expired but none had an easy time either.

When I got to camp, it didn't take long to figure out the important stuff. The first rule was that you wore mosquito repellant. Everywhere! In thick northern bush, next to a lake, the little pests would drive you insane. There was no stopping them except for this wonderful stuff known only as "bug juice."

Now and then we would be getting instruction while standing in formation and invariably someone would pick up a stick and tickle the person in front of them, making them think the little bastard mosquito hordes had gotten past their defenses. Just thinking about that now makes me cringe.

The second rule was that you kept your feet dry. Wet feet meant you got sick, were sent home in the middle of the camp and had to come back and take it over from the start.

After that, there were just the basics like remembering to fasten the top of the salt- and pepper-shakers before you used them because all of them had been loosened and gently placed on top again, ready to spill the contents at the slightest shake.

Then, there were the sins that kept you up all night. We had a cadet named Byers in our flight. While we were trying to get the few precious hours of sleep we could, Byers would act out stories from Star Wars or MacGyver or whatever TV show or movie he could think of that night, making it impossible for a lot of us to rest. It wasn't so bad that we didn't get enough sleep to replenish our bodies, it wasn't so bad that the poor guy was a little bit touched and no one liked him, it wasn't that the mosquito netting we used would let in the odd mosquito and drive us crazy. It was a combination of these things and the stress and competitiveness of the camp. Being one of the senior guys in my group, I took it upon myself to train a young Inuit boy named Ituk to hit Byers on command. It went something like this.

"Obi-Wan, I have you now!"
"Ituk! Hit him!"
Smack.
Silence.

It was a good game until we got caught. We didn't really get into trouble though, but it was funny seeing the look on Ituk's face when our sergeant was

Through The Withering Storm

standing right beside him while he stood on a lower bunk with his fist cocked. The little fellow actually thought if he hopped back into bed all would be forgiven. It was. No one really likes a guy who keeps everyone up at night, sergeants included.

One of the exercises we performed in our training included a search and rescue/downed aircraft scenario that took place in the vast areas of land that surrounded our camp. We were told there were survivors in a certain area and we were to go out, find them, administer first aid and we would be evaluated on our performance. Once again, you add me to this mix and you have a recipe for disaster. I don't know why, but often I just didn't care how far I had to go to accomplish a task. Though we were kids it didn't matter that I caused other people to risk injury or humiliation. It scares me almost to look back at those days and the things I would do. It was like I had no conscience.

It didn't take long to find the crash survivors. They were three cadets from the other flight and one of them had a real attitude problem. His job, as I am sure he was instructed, was to freak out and add an element of realism to our rescue.

"My wife! What happened to my wife!" he yelled continuously, while flailing around. This was fine when he was doing it to a girl who was in my flight. She simply tried to calm him down verbally and put up with his thrashings. But when it became my turn to sit with him, his antics started to really bug me, so I slapped him. Suddenly, a change came over him and he looked up at me.

"You f**king hit me again I'm going to kill you!" he shrieked. So, just for good measure, I hit him again figuring he'd shut up, calm down, end of story.

Wrong! He ended up raising so much trouble that even my close friends were considering turning me in. Luckily no one did, though, and I escaped without even a mark on my record. The funny thing about that camp was, no matter how much I resented it, the training really did me a lot of good. They didn't just train us how to survive a plane crash, they taught us first aid and how to hunt and trap animals, how to keep each other going, how to keep your mind strong. I keep thinking of this one time I saw an old man collapse in the street and another time when I saw a young boy get hit by a car, I was able to help, able to know what to do, because of this training.

There was another event that didn't sit well with my superior officers. There was one officer who I thought was a real slimy jerk. He was one of those guys who are in cadets to show off their superior social skills, especially for the female cadets (who were, as a rule, under age). I didn't like him much and it showed. One time, we were walking past him in formation and I put my hands together as though I was holding a pistol and pretended to shoot him. I saw it as a joke but my superiors saw it as insubordination. I got extra duties for that, but no marks on my record because that same officer was kicked out of the course a few days later for reading love letters containing explicit information to a class of cadets. I was more than pleased to hear about it.

Air Cadets was sometimes a silly game of playing soldiers but it was a fun game and a more grown-up game than most of us had ever played. Maybe I took it a little too seriously but the things I learned then have stayed with me my whole life. Back then, it seemed that the nickname "psycho" was given to me no matter where I went, no matter what course I was on.

Through The Withering Storm

To me, it seemed a good term, a title for someone so gung-ho he would do crazy things for ideals such as honor and justice. Jump in front of a bullet intended for someone else, throw yourself on a live grenade. Sadly though, being a psycho had little place in the real world aside from being a fictional main character of a somewhat entertaining movie. Inside me were the ideals my parents had tried to teach me, things like family and unconditional love, and outside were the things I did partly to show off, partly because I was mentally deteriorating as time went on. I thought I could make people laugh and make a name for myself so that I would be liked. I thought if I was feared I would be respected. All too often neither actions worked that way. In reality, I was longing to belong to the groups that formed in camps and school, longing to have a girlfriend and to care for someone. I just didn't know how to do that and I didn't want to show a weaker side of myself.

I didn't realize that an illness was eating away at my psyche and that the damage would surface one day like the great leviathan in Herman Melville's Moby Dick. What it came down to was the choice of go in after him or let the leviathan destroy me. My life wasn't all bad, I had some good times, some great times, family trips, drinking sessions with my dad, and some friends who watched out for me no matter how crazy I got. In many ways, I was an extremely lucky kid. In a few years though, when my behavior was no longer considered "acting out," and my problems became acute, I wasn't so lucky anymore.

As my time at camp wore on, the incessant rain we had that year and the long marches we had in it caught up to me and I came down with a serious flu. There was no way to really avoid it, I just wasn't going to let anyone know about it and get sent home.

I slogged through a few pretty difficult days of misery; I can barely remember them other than that at times I didn't have the strength to stand in formation. Eventually the flu went away and I was stronger for having held out. Soon after, it was time for us to shoulder our packs and head out into the wilderness. If only we had known what waited for us there.

We didn't think much of it at first. Our commanding officer didn't tell us we were going for five days, he just said we were going for a two-day exercise in the bush (as I was to learn later, he said the same to everyone) and off we went. The leaders hiked us out a long way, off on a track with a series of twists and turns, probably so we couldn't find our way back to camp on our own. Since the weather was terrible, they supervised us for a short while.

It was a total disaster. We couldn't find a source of clean water, couldn't get our fires lit, didn't have any way of drying our shelters and a lot of guys were near exhaustion from the hike. That meant they would all be sick the next day from the combination of fatigue and constant dampness. We ended up aborting the mission. So instead of a five-day test of our manhood, we had a one-day march, four days of movies, and exams upon exams, which were supposed to replace the real thing. I went home disappointed and, though I did learn a lot I could share with my squadron, this course was to be my last.

I got home and had nothing much to do for the rest of the summer, at least nothing special. On one of the first days back, my friend Lurch and I were riding our bikes in downtown St. Albert late at night, and we happened by a strip bar. Someone had left the door open in the July heat and I could see in. I was mesmerized. Somehow, seeing that attractive, unclothed woman marked the end of obsessing over

Through The Withering Storm

comic books and army clothes and the beginning of letting my hormones do the talking, letting myself be more of a normal teenager. I wish someone had told me then about how women can be the best friends you ever have and still be attractive and also be a life partner. The way I was introduced to the world of the opposite sex (as I am sure most 14-year-old boys are), I only saw women as sex objects, not the close friends and caring beings they are to me now.

For years to come, I would have an unhealthy concept of relationships and females. I suppose it could be traced back to seeing how my parents lived two separate lives, my mom suffering from her own mental illness which often hospitalized her in my younger years, and my dad denying any problem existed, drinking his nights away since his business folded in the mid 1980s. My difficult family life and the reverse polarity that a cadet was to other students in school made me stick out as an object of scorn and ridicule, at times even to other cadets. But I can remember the summer of 1986 as a turning point for me, a time when my focus really changed in life from lofty goals such as becoming an airline pilot, astronaut, or scientist, to desiring love and acceptance and good friends above all else. I was starting to grow up, though I had a long way to go.

The rest of that summer didn't add up to much, for two weeks I didn't have a best friend to hang out with because Lurch was off taking air crew survival in the third and final intake of the summer at the same camp I had been to. I spent a little time with my other buddies Frank and Jim. Lurch's crew had to go out on the five-day trek and it was funny hearing from him how our commanding officer had tears in his eyes when he said, "It broke my heart to lie to you guys about the five days."

I sent a little present up to camp for one of my favorite sergeants, Murray Mast. It was something he requested as our bus was leaving, wrapped in a plain brown bag. I told Murph to give it to him before kit inspection at the beginning of camp. It was one of the two magazines every cadet needs, the first being a quasi-legal journal for mercenaries, the second (which was what he got), a nudity mag I had stolen from my dad. To Murray, stuck there in the middle of the vast bush, it was pure gold.

The summer of 1986 slid by and, as sad as I was to see it go, part of me was excited about starting high school soon after. I had two advantages over the average grade 10 student. One was knowing an established group of friends in my new school, thanks to air cadets, and the other was knowing an established group of friends thanks to my brother Kris who was in the same school and going into Grade 11. No two groups could be farther apart. The cadets were rule-following, well-groomed honor students for the most part, and my brother's friends were often pot-smoking, party-going long-hairs or "heads" as we knew them.

The funny thing was that in a few years those group lines would become so blurred that few could tell them apart. Just as many had addictive personalities in both groups, just as many were successes in their chosen fields, and just as many were failures.

I was glad to have any friends in those difficult years. They were difficult not so much because of who I was but because of who I was becoming. My sister's boyfriend was starting to be a bigger influence on me, making me more socially and politically aware and less of a soldier willing to take orders. It was a fine line I walked. On one side, there

Through The Withering Storm

were the cadet parties, the drinking and the tougher classes that really accentuated the difference between the academics and the other students. On the other side, I was meeting people and knowing people who stood against the government and what the military did to young minds. Not to mention all the new responsibilities that came with growing up just a little bit more.

That, of course, didn't stop the traditional rites of passage. Twice, I was froshed as a Grade 10 student. Once, at a convenience store, when a jerk we called 'Carrot' threw an egg at me from 10 feet away for no reason. The second time, I was walking down a road and an egg seemingly came out of nowhere and smashed into my shoulder with enough force to nearly knock me down.

Not too many nights later, my brother and his friends got their hands on a truck and, since you had to be 18 to purchase eggs during frosh season, this long-haired, leather jacket-wearing friend of my brother went into a gas station and walked out with 10 cartons of eggs and got into the back of the truck with three other pals. I couldn't help laughing at the stupidity of the situation. It was obvious what 10 cartons of eggs would be used for but the gas station owner didn't care since he was making a sale. But I felt so wild and free to be a part of such a brazen, stupid stunt that I was giddy. Somehow I couldn't see then that by doing this I was as bad as the people in school who formed little groups for the main purpose of excluding others and feeling superior to them. Not to mention that it was really a nasty and destructive thing to do and if I were ever caught heads would have rolled.

We cruised around my home town for a while and couldn't find anyone stupid enough to be walking the streets during frosh season, so, at one point, we ducked down, armed ourselves with eggs and, as our truck went past a bus, we jumped up and slammed home a half dozen omelets' worth of eggs into the side of the big vehicle. Next, we conducted a revenge egging, tossing a few at the car of a fellow who had done some perceived wrong to one of our crowd. We even egged some people who were just out for a walk. We honestly believed that this was our one way of striking back at a world that sometimes didn't like us, often didn't want us, of evening up the rights and wrongs.

In school we pulled stunts, too, but nothing quite as harmful. We couldn't get away with it, being under constant supervision. As cadets at school, we always stuck together and, literally, had our own table in the lunchroom. There were two students at our table with whom I never got along, one because he was always spouting off about how rich his family was and another because he wasn't in air cadets with us. He was in army cadets and I didn't think he had earned the right to sit with us. It was mean, really, but the fact was, army cadets would do the same to us. As for the rich guy, he just drove me nuts. He was still a friend, though, just extremely annoying.

A short time into the Grade 10 year, I was with a couple of cadet buddies and we really wanted to get our hands on some beer. One of the guys was 18, which is the legal age to buy booze in Alberta, and the other was 16. The 18-year-old was scared to go in because he said some tough-looking guy lipped him off last time he was there and the 16 year-old didn't think he could get away with buying beer, so it all rested on my 14-year-old shoulders. I took the cash, went on into the bar, ordered and got my beer, and was ready to take off like a rabbit. But, on my way

Through The Withering Storm

out, someone said "Hi, Leif!" Some sort of a grunt came out of my mouth and I hurriedly made my exit. The next Monday at school I was the hero of my non-cadet school friends because it turned out it was one of their fathers who had seen me and didn't turn me in.

I had two favorite classes in Grade 10. One was social studies, and the other was physics. Social studies was the one class I would get out of bed for. Even if I had stayed up late drinking or was out of my mind tired from not sleeping because of one of my characteristic all night TV-watching sessions, I would get up, walk to school if I had missed the bus, and attend social studies. I suppose part of it had to do with an extremely attractive young woman in that class but, mostly, I liked it because it talked about the kind of stuff I was most interested in – politics.

I must have driven my teachers crazy that year because they would be trying to teach their mandatory curriculum, a touchy-feely version of the world around us, and I would be giving them second-hand accounts of war, revolution or tyranny as told to me by my dad or my sister's friends and boyfriend. They were often pretty whacked-out ideas from way left of center but a lot of them were true and verified. I often wonder what type of conversations came up in the teacher's lounge over the stunts I pulled and the things I said. I've contacted former teachers and some of them don't remember me, some had an inclination that I was headed off the deep end, and some of them wondered where I got some of the ideas and information I came up with. I was always up for an argument no matter how inconvenient the time or the place.

In social studies at one point we were tasked with setting up a political party of our own making and I started one with friends called 'The Conservative Rebels.' It was supposed to be a party that went against mainstream liberalism and back to grassroots conservatism. About that time, a real party was being formed that was just like it and, in later days, became very close to being elected as the governing party of Canada. Ironically, Preston Manning, the leader of the early 'Reform' party, had a daughter who was in my school at that same time.

What I didn't want my teachers to know at the time, though, was that while all this was going on my world was falling apart. I was a young and troubled kid, on the verge of becoming an alcoholic with a father who also drank to excess every day. Only a few months earlier, I had been incarcerated in a psychiatric ward but all the effort I put into hiding that only made things worse. The "psycho" tag followed me without prompting right into high school.

In the fall of my first high school year, around Halloween night, a friend and I decided we were going to get drunk and go to a dance. I knew that the only hope of getting me out on a dance floor was for me to be inebriated but this time I went a little too far. We got a friend to pick us up a 26-ounce (750mL) bottle of Canadian Whiskey, bought a two-liter bottle of coke for mix, and off we happily went to our dance. It wasn't far from my house to the cadet hall, where the dance was held, probably about three kilometers, which could easily be covered in about 40 minutes despite the snow, which was ankle-high on the paths and a bit more in the drifts.

I took it upon myself to consume most of the bottle, taking pride in the fact that I could drink a lot and handle myself when drunk. Halfway to the dance, the bottle was finished and so was I. All I can remember of that night was thrashing around in the

Through The Withering Storm

snow, seeing a mall in the distance and trying to make it there, knowing it would be warm and I could lie down and sleep there. I knew I was freezing, but I was unable to make my body work well enough to cover the distance. It was like swimming in mud.

My friend carried me as far as he could, but he was a skinny kid and could only get me about halfway. He propped me up sitting with my back to the mall parking garage and left me lying there while he went for help. Not one person in the whole damn squadron would come and help him so he came back on his own and there I was in the mall somehow, shouting out my phone number to a Good Samaritan who had somehow managed to get me inside. To this day, I have no recollection of it happening but apparently my parents came and got me and nearly had a fit. They ended up putting me to bed after taking off my clothes and I woke up in that state, about 15 hours later, naked and in my own bed.

I wonder if the man who helped me at the mall was my guardian angel or, if somehow I was meant to carry on my life past the age of 14 for some divine reason. Although I rarely ever did, I went to church that very next day and nursed my poor frozen feet. I would be unable to feel them for two more weeks.

Looking back, it was a pretty sick situation. I could tell I was destroying myself but it didn't hit home how I could change that. I didn't understand the need to make some major changes to my life or I would be headed for disaster. I was asking more and more from my weary young bones. For some reason I felt compelled to stay up all night, drinking to the limit, smoking cigars and cigarettes like they were going out of style, and still be fresh as a daisy to breeze through school as I always had, never taking home homework, just paying attention in class and leaving the rest up to my "superior" intellect. By spring, I was failing nearly every course, and was even close to being kicked out of school for all the absences that had been piling up.

Despite messing up in school, I still had an air cadet scholarship board to go to in order to be sent to my summer course of choice. This was going to be no picnic. They would examine me inside and out, everything from dress and deportment to squadron records and marks. This was one thing I couldn't screw up. If I did, my three years of being a model cadet would be over. I wouldn't be kicked out but would end up just another loser with no future except to wait for each year's new line of female cadets to hit on.

Our officers, who were all adults, prepared us well for our scholarship boards. We went through practice after practice and were given lists of all the important information to know. I did well in the mock-up sessions and, when the time came, I wasn't even nervous, having been fully prepared for what would happen. Three men sat in the barracks room – men who would decide my life for me. I remember every feeling, every emotion, even how the red door felt as my skinny knuckles knocked on it. I was invited in and sat down, just as I had been told. They asked me everything from what I did in my free time to my thoughts on seatbelt legislation. I had been reading newspapers for a while to keep current, so when they asked me about the legislation, I started quoting figures from Australia on traffic deaths. Then, they asked me the kicker.

"Who is the director of Camp Wainwright?" came the question. I drew a blank. I didn't think it was all that bad, having answered every other question.

"I'm sorry, sir, I do not know the answer to that question," I said, in the manner we were taught to use when an answer eluded us. The board member in the middle of the panel ruffled his tie a bit, moved around his nameplate and asked me again:

"Are you sure you don't know the answer to the question?"

"Yes, sir, I am sorry but I do not know the answer to that question."

There was a bit of a tense pause and then one of the other members spoke up.

"Well, we have looked at your records. It's obvious that you are a credit to your country. I guess you can go now," he said.

I escaped down the hall and grabbed a sheet from someone that included the list of the important names we were supposed to memorize. The person who had asked me the troubling question was the answer to the query. The correct reply should have been "Bud Worthington", and he had been sitting right in front of me. When we got the results back, I was put on the reserve list for the course but I guess no one ever cancelled out or got sick. I missed the course and, with that, put an end to my cadet career.

I was still sent to a camp but it was just a five-day session in the woods with a bunch of civilians, nothing like the blood-and-guts course I was supposed to have taken. Thinking back, I seriously doubt they rejected me because of the failed memorization of a name. There is little doubt that it was actually because of my poor school records. I had gone from being an honor student in Grade 8 to nearly dropping out of high school in Grade 10.

Those last few days of that first term were the hardest. I thought somehow I could pull myself out of the downward slide but everything was a mess. I was no longer a top-level cadet and I was no longer a top achiever in school. I actually had believed that, no matter what, this sort of thing couldn't happen to me. I remember going from class to class being astounded that I could have done so poorly. The marks came in – fail, fail, fail   There was no such thing as repeating a grade in the Alberta system in high school, which was perhaps a good thing. You had to repeat the courses you failed and you could progress in the ones you didn't. I failed more than half my courses and, in the next two more years of school, couldn't manage to pick up that missing chunk of my education. The only positive thing that came out of that year was that I was about to take a serious look at my life. Unfortunately, the tragic aspect of my decision to change my life is that none of those changes would have much effect on the cruel joke nature had already played on me – and the worst was yet to come.

Through The Withering Storm

Chapter Three: From Bad to Worse

That summer, partly because I was one of the few cadets who didn't have a course at that time and mostly because my dad was organizing it, I took on a big role in the Canada Day celebrations which consisted of a parade and all-day festivities in St. Albert's Lion's Park on July 1. I had the honor of leading the parade dressed up in a three-piece suit carrying the Canadian flag. As soon as the parade finished, I rushed home to change and then came back for more fun.

I was employed for the rest of that day as a messenger and was given the use of a quad, which was far too powerful and noisy for a small park. That was the last year the event organizers ever used a quad at the park because not only did I not know how to shift gears on the thing, I didn't really have much experience driving. As a result, the machine tore around at full tilt everywhere I went, cutting off foot racers at one point, and angering a father who implored me to give his daughters a ride. That was the way I did everything back then – full tilt and damn the torpedoes. And why not? I was 15 and convinced I was invincible at that age. Everyone knows bad things don't happen to reckless kids!

The day finished up with a spectacular fireworks display and many people agreed it was the best Canada Day celebration St. Albert had ever seen. We even had cooperation from the military with a few paratroopers landing in the park. In the morning when we had all gathered to sing O Canada, right at the height of the song a four-engine C-130 Hercules came roaring over the park so low it removed more than one hat. Even though I was turning away from the military at that age, I still swelled with pride when that happened. It blew everyone away and was a total surprise to everyone but my dad, who had helped organize it.

The next day I was scheduled to work at MacDonald's and my arms and face were sunburned so badly I could barely stand in front of the fryer without being in pain. After a manager looked at me and had a bit of a laugh, I was sent out into the lobby to clean tables. It was obvious I wasn't faking the pain. A lot of people think that working in a place like that would be the worst job possible but it was actually one of the better jobs I have had. There were a lot of nice girls working there and I managed to get my very first date with one of them. There were even a few girls who weren't so nice but still could be a lot of fun. One of those girls ended up selling me her Moped; along with other small favors she kindly supplied me for free.

Before too long, my Air Cadet course date came up and my dad dropped me off at the bus depot to meet the other air cadets who were on the course with me. I don't know if I made a good impression on them, but in the first couple of hours while we were waiting for someone from the Air Cadet League, I decided to take them on a tour of Edmonton and we went for a beer. It didn't matter to me that I was only 15. I had the money and was thirsty so off we went.

My dad drove us up to the camp itself when the time came to go. The course took place in a provincial park near Hinton, Alberta. You couldn't ask for a more beautiful place to drive to in the summer. The trees, the lakes, the hills, the mountains, the crisp air and the open road. This route eventually led to Jasper – a place that represented freedom to me.

Through The Withering Storm

Jasper was a special place where my family always seemed to work well together and everyone got along. It was a great respite from the frigid winter nights when my dad would drink, my sister would escape to her room to read or go out to participate in one of her many church activities. My Mom would just hide. My brother would hide, too, I guess. He was forever downstairs lifting weights. In Jasper though, we were all together all the time and we were happy to be in one of the most beautiful places in the world.

On the first day of the camp, we all gathered in a meeting hall and I noticed what was going to take over my attention for the rest of the time I was there. Her name was Karen and she was beautiful — slim and pretty, with freckles and long, curly brown hair. I didn't really think Ihad a chance with her but still approached her and we became friends. She was easy to talk to, sweet and extremely intelligent with a great sense of humor. I was smitten. I wouldn't have carried such a torch for her except that a few days later she did something that made me think she liked me back.

On this particular day, our training group was split up and my half of the group was told to play a game. The group on the upper floor was given colored cards and told the object was to collect as many as possible. The group on the lower floor was told to approach people and make them feel happy and comfortable. I was sent from the top floor, where I didn't care much about the card game, to join the group downstairs, not knowing what game they were playing. Karen came up and put her arm around me, asking how I was doing and saying all these nice things. From that point on, she could have emitted toxic waste and I still would have been nuts about her.

I even asked her on a date to see the latest James Bond movie and she agreed, but we ended up losing touch after the camp was over. She was on my mind constantly after I got home, to the point of obsession, which was not healthy for me.

The camp itself was superb. We did a lot of exercises that were meant to foster good leadership and self discovery. There were canoe trips, rock climbing outings, hikes in the hills and even an obstacle course. I had felt horrible that summer because of my grades, the impending end of cadets and the loss of a lot of friendships. But Blue Lake Camp was the bright jewel in the garbage pile my life had become. Thinking back now and it possibly saved my life.

While I was working at MacDonald's, I met one of the first good friends I ever had who wasn't a cadet. His name was Dan Reilly and he was a terribly nice guy. He had moved up to St. Albert from a small town called Dunn and he would do anything for a laugh. While I weighed around 160 lbs., he was more than 200 lbs. and well over six feet tall. It was kind of funny to see him stuff himself into his little Honda Civic which took us all over the place that summer. He even taught me how to drive a car with a standard transmission.

At one point during the summer, the store we worked in took us to Sylvan Lake, a popular central Alberta vacation spot, for a company picnic. Dan kept bumming money off me and others to ride the water slides and I had gotten a friend, who was over 18, to buy me a bunch of booze which left me a little more than tipsy.

I had some funny ideas about life at that time; I used to 'practice' drinking while I watched TV late at night. One of my first sessions was with a bit of

Through The Withering Storm

rum, a bit of cola and a gravy boat. I felt almost nothing except a sick kind of pride of being man enough to drink alcohol. Apparently, people with bipolar disorder, with which I had been diagnosed in the hospital, are five times more likely to become alcoholic than others. Like my favorite Drill Sergeant used to say, I was swimming up a river of shit with no paddle and no boat. I couldn't function in my normal life smoking and drinking and I couldn't ever get up any courage to have any kind of social or sex life without them. Smoking too was a social lubricant because I got to be friends with all the 'heads' that went out to smoke on breaks.

      Not long after I first tried alcohol, I was getting invited to drinking parties or plotting to get my hands on some booze with friends. Beer and I had a strange relationship. A couple of beers would make me feel good, kind of happy and loosen me up so I could do things like rub up against some poor girl at a dance. But just one too many made me feel like I would rather be dead. I would throw up, pass out and run around screaming. I had a devil inside me and though I don't know if I ever managed it, I kept on believing that I could find that proper middle ground where the beast was tamed and I felt good. It was literally insanity, doing the same thing again and again expecting to get different results.

After I had finished drinking my booze at the staff summer party, I thought it would be funny to get some people together to throw one of our managers into the lake. I tried to rally some troops, and at first it seemed like they were all coming with me until I got in close and looked back to see I was alone in my efforts. The manager put me into a wrestling throw and I instinctively reversed it, landing on top of him. After that we didn't see him for a while and when we did, he was on crutches. I think I would have been fired if it weren't for the fact that I was half his size and it couldn't be proven I was the aggressor even though I was. That wasn't even the only time I was to seriously injure someone while I was drunk.

My friend Dan was quite the life of the party that summer. I remember him switching cars from his Honda Civic to a 1978 Mustang and putting in a special horn that would play everything from the Star Wars anthem to the distinctive honk of the Dukes of Hazzard. He also had a CB radio with a speaker set up on the outside of his car that he would use to do things like order extra hamburgers from the person in front of him at the drive-through window or use his lame pick up lines on women he saw. Dan is also still a close friend today and he hasn't stopped being a funny guy or being a nice guy. In one of the supreme ironies of my life, every vice I had back then, so it seems, Dan participates in now, and he was one of the people most instrumental in getting me to curb my appetites.

Eventually, that summer ended and I tried to make some positive changes in my life. New friends outside of cadets, a new work ethic at school, and I even tried to put a cap on my drinking (but not by total abstinence). I was about to start Grade 11 and I was lost somewhere between left and right, childhood and adulthood, good and bad.

Since the end of grade 10 spelled the end of cadets for me, I made a decision that I wanted two things; — a car and better grades. There was no way I could attain either goal with the time demands of air cadets so I simply quit. It was the easy thing to do at the time but an extremely hard choice to live with. Leaving cadets, no matter how much I hated marching and being picked on at school because of my loyalty, left a huge hole in my life.

As did many of my regrets, they would surface when I slept, in the form of nightmares of a nature most foul. I would dream about the friends I had, the girls I had crushes on, and that I was still at the top of my game. They weren't average snakes and ravens' nightmares, but they were added to my insomnia, headaches and poor health, so they ended up being extremely scary. But in truth, nightmares are a kind of fiction for people who sleep poorly. As in this and many other parts of my life, the truth would one day soon far outpace the dreaming world in terms of creating fear and emotional pain. I didn't know how it was going to happen, but some day soon the rug would be pulled out from under me and I would make a quick, brain-splitting trip to the hard cold floor.

Blue Lake camp ended, the summer sun slowly giving way to cool winds and leaves turning yellow on the trees. I looked forward to my grade 11 year but still harbored some sadness that I didn't connect with Karen. Then, school started and, for the first time in four years, air cadets didn't start for me.

It left me feeling somewhat empty, not joining up with all those people I had gotten to know so well over the years. I soon realized I missed hearing the stories about what people had done at camp, which instructors were back, and which officers were humiliated. I was determined to make a clean break from cadets, though, to not associate with any of them and to not look back.

Too many times I had seen guys, who never wanted to grow up, stay in cadets when they really weren't learning anything or doing much more than socializing. I hadn't completely given up the idea of joining the Canadian Forces, but a big part of me wanted to put cadets behind me.

Sometimes, when I think of that time of my life, I see myself as a cold person who deserved not to have friends, but, perhaps, I was just trying to save myself from the humiliation that I constantly felt. It often seemed I was barely one step ahead of it.

My two best friends, just before summer, told me flat out they were pulling the plug on our friendship and I was devastated. They never said much to me about their decisions. One sent a message through another friend and the other just walked up and told me: "I don't want to hang out with you anymore." I couldn't really understand why but I think it had to do with my views of the world. I was the centre of the universe and everyone else had to accept that. Looking back now, it probably started with little things — how I would pick on a fellow who sat at our lunch table in school, my complaining about them not letting me drive their cars so I could pass my driver's license test, and concluded with the insanity they saw in me, while drinking. At one point, I had actually broken one of these two friends' collarbone by jumping on him when I was drunk. There were many other incidents, some of which were related in this book, and some of which I don't want to delve into, and, then, of course, the ones I don't remember.

All this further compounded the devastation I felt about losing my cadet buddies in my final days with that group. So, my theory with friends became: instead of waiting for others to do the same hurtful thing again, I took the first step and cut them off completely whenever I had the chance. Needless to say, it didn't make for many lasting friendships in my young life.

Through The Withering Storm

Another factor working against my quest for popularity was that I saw myself as an academic at heart, and really wanted to return to that persona from previous years. I didn't want to make another horrible showing like I had in grade ten. Little did I know this would prove to be an impossible task.

I had to make some hard decisions that year as I was determined to make it into university. Setting up my course schedule so that I would re-take some of the courses I previously failed, I took a double spare so as to have time to do the massive amounts of homework I was determined to complete.

The two guys from my junior high school days seemed like good people to me at the time. They were gun nuts and, often, we would go out after school and do silly things such as lining up toy soldiers and blowing them away with shotguns, or driving down back roads at night and using speed limit signs for target practice. In truth, they were deeply disturbed youths, both much older than me and headed for a difficult life. I can recall one of them stating that none of us would ever amount to anything except his little sister. I couldn't allow him to lump me in like that and clearly stated that I, too, was going somewhere with my life, whether they were or not.

Still, they were friends and I tried my best to be their friends. I was not that socially skilled and I suppose I came across as arrogant and cruel. After talking for a while with Pat, he said something that made me step back and take a look at how vindictive and backstabbing I was at the time. We were running down a list of flaws of the other member of the group, Ralph. Pat said, "Isn't it odd that two intelligent grown people can't think of anything to talk about other than what's wrong with Ralph." That hit home.

I suddenly saw myself doing something I despised in other people. I was running down someone to deflect the focus from my increasing flaws and myself. I caught a glimmer of what I was starting to realize was a superiority complex that would dog me for many years and cause me no end of trouble and heartache. I did get good grades and I did have the ability to work hard and learn tasks quickly but, ever since I was a small boy, there was something wrong. Perhaps, it was with the way I saw the world or the way I felt. There was no way for me to identify it. I just knew there was just something mentally wrong with me.

What I can recall from a very early age was something I have heard mirrored by others that suffered from these same problems. I laid in my parent's bed and looked up at a family picture, and somehow got the impression that there were two families, one that was there when I was young and happy, and another that was there as part of some grand conspiracy with me at the center. Two distinctly different realities.

Although I had quit air cadets, when school started again, I didn't quit my part-time job at McDonald's. I really liked the idea of having money of my own and the independence it gave me. The beginning of the end came with one manager who used to ask me for cigarettes all the time. One day, I told him off and he apologized and gave me money for a pack. Then, when I had bought the pack, he asked to borrow another cigarette. He was one of these people that try to cut down by only smoking OPs (other people's).

When school started, he thought he would do me a favor by giving me full-time shifts. Something about my personality, maybe my lack of solid friendships let me be taken in by guys like this. Now, my schedule was even worse than with air cadets and I didn't know any way of saying no. With the shifts this manager gave me, I would be up at 7 a.m., go to school until 3 p.m., head to my job and work until 11 p.m., and then somehow make my way home.

The stress was incredible and I started to get lax about work and bend the rules now and then. Eventually, I got caught lying about when I started my shift, mostly because I was so tired I just wanted a break for a cigarette and a pop. I was sent home as punishment.

I actually liked the manager who caught me. She was a nice person and usually gave people a fair shake. When she sent me home, she told me that she wouldn't work with someone who lied to her, which made me feel horrible. She had found out from another manager that I hadn't worked long enough for a third break. Now, as I look back, I wish I hadn't lied, but there is kind of an odd hypocrisy in North America that deals with the subject of lying. On television, in movies, even in songs, lying is glorified. Lying is seen as an efficient way to get your desired result.

I can't claim that as an excuse, but feel it was a factor in me often lying at that age, combined with the fact that I had very little guidance, other than perhaps my sister who had problems of her own, having left the family a while back and left the church teachings behind to live with her communist boyfriend. I was left in a moral void and I am pretty sure now that it had to do with the fact that I never had good close friends or lasting relationships.

I also think lying was a big part of me hiding who I was deep down inside, trying to protect myself from becoming a complete social outcast. I was being worked to death for a tiny salary, despite my bosses knowing my schooling would suffer. Still, in this instance my conscience ate me alive.

The next day I was too embarrassed to go in and face up to what I had done so I didn't go in at all and I was fired. It was the worst feeling in the world and I remember going to my dad with tears in my eyes, thinking I had let him down. He said he didn't feel that way at all and that he was actually kind of proud of me for sticking things out under such circumstances. I had gone to work at the low end and survived for five months. In a short while, I was relieved to have time to study and focus on my grades full-time. I just had to give up the new albums and $5 lunches since quitting drinking or smoking wasn't an option.

It was around this time that I started hanging out with a couple of guys who were more along the lines of who I envisioned myself to be. Their names were Travis and Stan. Stan was Danish and a fairly smart guy and Travis was his best friend. They got good grades and had jobs at a car wash which Travis' dad owned. What I liked best about them was that they had the work ethic like the one that had run through my family for so many generations. Work first, then friends, then beer.

Not long after we met, Stan and Travis helped me get me a job in the same car wash and the three of us spent most of our days together for a few months and stayed friends for the rest of high school. Working at the car wash was hard, but in a way we loved it because we were all car-crazy at that age. The three of us worked together four days a week wiping down cars as they came through the end of the line of hoses and brushes. A small bonus was that we drove the cars out and parked them after they were

Through The Withering Storm

done. Over the next few months, Travis, Stan, a friend from junior high, Will Stuart, and I would share many good and bad times and a lot of beer with each other.

The car wash was an interesting place to work. There were a lot of alcoholic jerks working there who only cared about sex, drugs and alcohol. The cheaper the better and, at that particular time, Travis, Stan and I fit right in, except for the fact that the three of us lived in the suburbs with our parents and were all virgins. Back then, Stan had a red 1972 GMC truck that was so fast the G-forces it created when he stepped on the gas reminded me of my gliding days in cadets. Stan was a really competitive guy. He somehow felt that by having a faster vehicle meant you were better than other people and that they would be jealous. I had fun riding in his truck but I didn't care which car was faster. It was actually pretty dangerous to ride with him because he didn't seem to have much control over what he was doing.

To pass the time at the car wash, we played video games and poker for dimes. I was mired in this world of working for very little, spending what I had on beer and cigarettes, and there didn't seem to be much I could do about it. I remember my Mom coming in to wake me one time and I was so tired from whatever activity I had engaged (or imbibed) in the night before that I might as well have just gotten an electric shock treatment. I was starting to think I would never get a break. Stay in school, work hard, work hard after school, get into university, work hard and get good grades, then find a good job and work hard…it never seemed to end. And, it scared me that I would never get a day off or a break long enough to even feel rested.

Add to that I was having more bitter fights with my dad, mostly when he had been drinking. Most of these arguments started while we were at the supper table, generally over politics. It was around that time that my mom and I started going to Alanon, the group meetings for families and loved ones of alcoholics. Going to the meetings didn't last but it made things a little better at home. My dad was starting to look at his destructive behavior differently. It made no change in my own drinking, though. But, it did begin to germinate a seed.

Because I had scraped by with a passing mark the year before, I had made it to grade eleven physics, though I had yet to complete any high school math. Derek, who I knew from cadets, was in my class. He was a bit nerdy and, each day when I walked into class, I would grab a jar of cockroaches in formaldehyde and threaten to toss it at him (our physics class took place in a biology lab). I would toss it at him and he would catch it, day after day. Then, one day, he sat there and said to me, "I'm not going to catch it this time."

"Well, I'm going to throw it!" I said.

He didn't waver. I threw it and it smashed on the floor, sending oversized cockroaches everywhere.

"Derek! Clean that up!" our teacher yelled at him.

"I didn't do it, it was Leif!" he replied.

"Both of you clean it up! Now!"

I complied with her request, only I left a few surprises around the room. I put a cockroach on a chair and then pushed the chair under a desk and left a few on Derek's books and then rolled one up in paper towel and stuffed the roll back into the wall dispenser. The trick came off beautifully later that day.

Through The Withering Storm

Apparently, a young woman came in, pulled out her chair and screamed her head off.

Always the hero, my buddy Will Stuart happened to be there and he said: "Oh, don't worry. I'll pick it up for you!" and began to crank the dispenser handle to get some paper towel. Nothing came out and he decided to pull the paper out himself when a second cockroach seemingly jumped out of the dispenser and landed on his chest, causing him to scream like a girl.

As far as the humiliation factor went, this was even better than the time I loosened the top of a salt shaker at a restaurant table and my brother ruined an eight-ounce steak by falling for the oldest cadet trick in the book. My dad nearly killed me. When I was pulling a prank, I never seemed to consider what kind of effect it had on people. It was one thing to ruin a steak at a cadet function, when we were getting our food for free, but I would pull a prank like this on my own family, knowing full well I would be caught and punished.

The weird thing is that I don't really know if this was a symptom of mental illness or simply that of a careless teenager. I do know that once I saw an opportunity to cause problems for people, I would grab it and do my worst. I have heard of something called "poor impulse control," a term Sigmund Freud coined meaning that basically if I wanted something (in those dark days of my youth) it was very hard to refuse this desire for any length of time. This can be combined with other factors such as how I would compulsively collect comic books and, before that, stamps and coins and toy soldiers and any number of objects. I even had early signs of gambling and alcohol addiction.

At this point in my life, I was starting to become someone who really wasn't the person my family once knew. I was becoming a selfish, destructive young adult.

Thanksgiving came and went, Halloween came and went, both not meaning much to me. I was too old to 'trick or treat' and too young to find a date for a dance or party. November followed and it was time to head back into the mountains for the second half of the Blue Lake course I had taken in the summer.

I had explained to my former commanding officer that I was no longer in cadets and didn't think it was fair that I take the course at the cost to the Department of National Defense, but he said I earned it and so I went proudly. The course had little meaning to me, other than it was my last official duty as an air cadet and that I would see Karen who had agreed to go out with me but had never called. She was there, beautiful as ever, and met me with a short apology. After a long talk, we went up to the camp on the bus and I was in love again. As I look back now, trouble was brewing with me and something was desperately wrong. During the first half of the camp, I had stayed in a full cabin of four and we kept each other up late with stories of drinking and our hometowns and girls.

But, when the second part of the camp came around, I didn't have any friends and so everyone else moved out of my cabin. All of them had made friends with people in other cabins and I reasoned if I were on my own I would sleep better. In fact it made me feel horrible to be alone, knowing I didn't have a friend in the world at home or here at camp. Not to mention that insomnia had dogged me for a long time. I remember lying there, wired like I had inhaled 100

Through The Withering Storm

cups of coffee, completely unable to sleep, depressed about everything in my life and experiencing a mania with thoughts of Karen running full tilt through my head while she was not 100 feet away in another cabin. I would finally drift off in the early morning hours and then drag my smoker's skinny frame into the meeting hall, make a cup of tea, eat an orange, in no shape to face the day.

This time, before I left camp I made sure to get Karen's phone number and for the next few months I would put everything I had into trying to charm her into my life. She was a sweet girl and we did meet up a few times but I was no competition for the older and more mature guys she had been dating (she was two years my senior, a lifetime in high school years). The first time we met up was at West Edmonton Mall, she broke my heart by bringing her friend (who I couldn't stand). For some reason, she wanted to see a romantic movie so the three of us watched Dirty Dancing with Patrick Swayze (oddly enough, I stood within three feet of this same actor at this same mall years later.) Another time, we met up at a mall near her school and went driving around her neighborhood looking at all the big expensive houses. We had one final date when we met at a restaurant on Jasper Avenue in downtown Edmonton. That was the last I saw her. A few weeks later when I called her house, her dad answered and told me to give up on her. I was left with this terrible sense of intruding on her happiness so I decided never to call again. The big problem was that I couldn't stop thinking about her.

That year, I stayed up late a lot and would try to make up for that by having a short nap after school. I would have the worst dreams during these afternoon naps. A tiger would jump out of my closet to devour me. I dreamt I was old and near death and my life had been a waste. The dreams were frightening but the reality was worse. I was caught in the middle of untreated mental instability and, when I would wake up, I would think of Karen. She was the key to the happiness I could never have. It was a time of desperation.

At school, my English course was a lot of work but my hard work paid off. As one of the plays we were to study, our teacher had chosen Macbeth. I had a strong literary background, had already read a few plays and, by a stroke of luck, some really attractive girls were in my study group. I talked of love and honor and betrayal to them in words they could understand and I think it left an impression on at least one of them. It was one of the best times I had ever had in school and, from then, on I had top marks in English.

I still did a lot of crazy things and I didn't care much about my own safety or sanity. I even had trouble keeping my clothes washed, my hair combed and my teeth brushed. I was way off kilter and no gag was too big to pull. Once again, no matter what I changed or where I went, the old "Psycho" tag came with me. One night in particular, I was with my friend Will. We had been drinking heavily and walking around St. Albert well after dark. It was 1988 and the Calgary Winter Olympic Games were on. I never saw athletes as young fit people worthy of admiration. I saw 'jocks' as the enemy.

Athletes were the guys who bullied you, the guys who punished the intelligent because they were better at academics. The Olympic flame had come through town and a tall torch, burning bright at the town hall, had been erected in its honor. My mission? Light a cigarette on the Olympic flame, making a

Through The Withering Storm

statement about what I thought of sports in general. I succeeded in my mission that night, but there was one small problem — I got caught. I had no trouble climbing up the 15-foot structure, and no problem lighting my cigarette, but, just as I was to let myself, down a voice came booming from behind that said, "It is extremely dangerous to light a cigarette from the Olympic flame!" It was a security guard behind me. Of course, my witness was laughing at the whole thing, hidden 100 feet back. I simply got down, puffed on my cigarette, apologized, and, wavering slightly, made my way out of there with another crazy story to tell.

About this same time, I had got myself a really good job at IGA in my hometown. I had impressed the manager and he gave me one of the preferred jobs in the bakery. Three days a week, I would go in and spend four hours cleaning and dusting and scrubbing pans and sweeping and mopping. I loved it. I did my work without supervision and, by the end of my shift, the place was spotless.

One of the girls from my English class got a job in the deli right across from where I worked. She was a tall, slim, ambitious girl who cared a lot about her appearance. She had the most beautiful curly blonde hair and a smile that could light up a warehouse. She could have made me forget all about Karen but I was too nervous and shy to come out of the shell I was hiding in. I stayed in the bakery all the time while I was at work, and soon after I started there, due to some cost-cutting measures, I lost my job. It was a big blow to lose that job and I knew I would have a hard time finding another one that would pay the same. I faced the coming summer with no girlfriend, no job and, perhaps, worst of all, no friends to speak of. Even Stan, Will and Travis were beginning to lose interest in being friends with me. Not long before the end of school, I tried to explain to them the advantage of moderating one's drinking without explaining to them that I was going to Alanon meetings with my mom and that I didn't want to end up as an alcoholic. They took personal offence to my suggestions. I didn't talk with them again until school started in the fall. It never helps to think too much about what 'could have been.' The fact is my life then, and in times to come, was a long series of revolving door friendships and employment.

Before the end of Grade 11, one more memorable event occurred when one of my gun-nut friends held a party at his house that coincided with a party his sister was having. I ended up half drunk, walking arm in arm with two beautiful girls and, later, eating pizza and watching old karate movies on TV with the whole crew. It felt like everything was falling into place for me. I was starting to get over Karen and I had met these really cute girls. I was starting to feel liked and attractive and I wasn't stuck in the same old cadet circles. I was making genuine friends of my own.

A couple of days later I called up my friend's house and asked his sister out on a date. He had said time and again that he was cool with me dating her, so I went right ahead and asked her. She said yes and I could hardly wait for the day to come. That Friday, I took her to a movie, drove her around the countryside, and took her to McDonald's for supper. Then the moment of truth came and I walked her up to the driveway of her house. I went to kiss her on her cheek but I felt her mouth open as mine came near, so I moved in and gave her a full French kiss. It was the best feeling I ever had and I was elated that night on the way home.

A couple of days later I phoned her up but she said she was busy on the nights I wanted to take her out. I told her brother to tell her she could call me or not call me, whatever she liked. As the days went by and she didn't call, I slipped into a deep depression again. I came pretty close to wanting to kill myself by driving my car at full speed into a building. I had no idea why she didn't call, why she kissed me like that if it was a goodbye kiss. I have thought about it a thousand times and the only thing I can think of was that she didn't like my junky old truck but even that seems ridiculous.

St. Albert was a small town and the communication lines were always buzzing. Someone could have talked to this girl's parents and put a stop to our seeing each other. I have a suspicion these 'communication lines' were often what kept me from finding a girlfriend. My only evidence is that every time I went to a small town I had no problems meeting and doing things with the opposite sex. For a while. But, where I was known, there was just no chance. What really hurt was that I didn't know any of this and I didn't understand any of it at the time. I just thought I was a piece of garbage and that was that.

One by one that spring, I lost all the friends I had. Even my old cadet buddies were either too busy to hang out with me or had girlfriends or, in the case of one of them, had run away from home. The months that followed that time are almost too painful to remember. Slowly my mind and body was being taken over by a beast that would one day claim possession of my soul. There was nothing I could do to fight it. I couldn't study harder, I couldn't be nicer to my dad, and I couldn't be a better employee or a better churchgoer. It was coming and, by the summer of 1988, it was gaining on me, ready to swallow me whole.

Through The Withering Storm

Chapter Four: Monster on the Horizon

Grade 11 ended and so did my whole social life. As a 16-year-old, this was like being beaten with a nightstick and having lit cigarette butts put out on your back. So many people my age were having their first relationships, partying with their friends, spending a summer out at a lake or at a cadet course. I was stuck with only my parents to talk to and I felt like I could not reveal to them how I was slipping into a deep cloud of near-desperation and depression. I didn't want to admit any weaknesses – especially any that could put me back in a mental ward. Another factor was that I didn't really know anything was wrong. I had problems with friends, I had problems with girls, I had problems with sleep and drinking, but when they were all considered separately, it didn't seem like there was any one single thing that caused my depression. It was at this stage, I realized I wanted to talk with a psychiatrist but hadn't a clue about where to start.

To top off my problems of loneliness and isolation, just as school let out, my car broke down. I was no longer working at the IGA so I had no money to take the car to a mechanic or even afford to keep it running, once it was fixed. I ended up taking an extremely low-paying job at a pizza joint on the main street of St. Albert, cooking pizzas and making dough. The high point of my day was finishing work, walking to the corner store for a pop and saying hi to the attractive young girl working behind the counter. Then, I would walk the two kilometers home and stay up all night once again, watching endless TV programs, fattening myself up with hot dogs, smoking my parents' cigarettes and trying to make up for all the unhealthy behavior by doing my nightly martial arts workout.

Not wanting to spend any money (especially since I had so little) on my car, I got a book from the library that was written for my make and model, and went to work on my old Dodge by myself. After a lot of reading and some trial and error, I found the problem, fixed it, and to my amazement the old beast roared to life. This was one of the few times I really felt good that whole summer, when my car roared to life because of the work of my own two hands. I hadn't solved any of my other problems, but, now, at least, I had some freedom. I scanned the classified ads and found myself a much better job than I had, delivering pizza in Edmonton. I didn't even go back for the scant pay my pizza-making job in St. Albert had promised.

My first few days working as a delivery person in the big city were frustrating to say the least. Edmonton is based on a system of streets going north-south and avenues going east-west. The first couple of days were spent in an area called Mill Woods, where you would often have addresses that were on 23rd street and 20th avenue. Being a little sketchy on the whole system didn't help. I would go out with an order and end up searching for the address for an hour. Then, at the end of the day I would have to drive for half an hour to get home, to the other side of the city. Since I was paid by how many deliveries I had made, plus tips if I got there fast enough, until I learned the street grid properly, I made very little money and was near the end of my rope trying to make ends meet. It was stressful and difficult, but I liked the idea of eating pizza every night, having free pop, and doing nothing really but driving.

Through The Withering Storm

I stuck with the job, even though I can remember sometimes waiting hours between orders and just sitting and staring at a blank wall. That never bothered me. I always had a lot to think about and often it was about Karen from camp the year before and the few dates I had with her. I was torturing myself really, but, in some kind of screwed up way, when a person is clinically depressed they actually take comfort in such self-punishing activities.

I remember the deep sadness that was beginning to fill my heart and mind. It was probably a combination of my loneliness for friends as well as a romantic partner, combined with some kind of genetic predisposition I had. I remember seeing pairs of people, a man and woman or two women, walking along the street and feeling so horrible that they had friends, someone to share their thoughts and desires, and all I had were my parents and my car.

When I was in that kind of funk, I seriously doubt if having a million friends would have made a difference. The sadness was in me, not in connecting with people. I needed treatment from a professional and I wasn't aware of the depth of my despair. Of course, it hurts to lose friends, but if I had caught my problem earlier, like when I was 14 at the hospital, I honestly think that I could have had a shot at a much more normal life. Maybe, I would not have such a demanding and aggravating personality that drove a wedge between others and me, not the least of whom was my dad.

I was to learn later that other people who delivered pizza would often take their buddies with them and have a party in the car, doing all kinds of crazy things for fun. After a while, my boss told me I was one of his fastest drivers and I knew I was making good money, but it all seemed so pointless. I was making money to buy gas and fix my car so I could make more money to buy more gas and fix my car some more. I wasn't saving up for a trip with friends or a date or anything. I was just running in a little rat's maze and getting nowhere fast.

One day, around the middle of summer, my mom sent me to the library. While looking through the books, I found a copy of the satanic bible. Out of curiosity, I checked it out and looked through it a bit. There were all kinds of stories and incantations in other languages and I didn't think much of it. In fact, at the time, I professed to be a staunch atheist, not believing in any form of spiritual existence. One day though, a week or so later, I got a phone call from a girl I knew in school who said she wanted to meet me at one of the local make-out locations. I was surprised but felt pretty happy.

I went up to a place we called "Man-made Lake" and there she was – only she was dressed up like a prostitute. She said that she had seen some cops and that we had to go over to the edge of the lake and talk. I considered whether I should drive off and leave her there but, for some reason, I trusted her.

I had heard from many people, including my brother, that she was a pretty messed up person and to be careful. When we got around to the side of the lake, we sat down on some steps, she started rubbing my leg. Everything seemed pretty weird and she looked scared. Then, she started asking me if I wanted to sleep with her and I tried to avoid the question. She kept insisting and finally I said, "Okay, yes, I want to sleep with you but…" Just as I said 'but' I felt the fury of her fist hitting the side of my face and laughing and yelling coming from the surrounding trees. She had set me up.

Through The Withering Storm

It was just a cheap prank. I walked back to my car and I could see the group of them, the gun-nuts and whoever else, walking out of the woods, having a great time at my expense. I could have easily pulled the rifle out of my car and put the fear of God into them, or even killed one or two, but with all the moral training I had gleaned from my family and some church attendance, that option was the last thing on my mind.

Instead, I just drove home and swallowed the pain of being led to think I was someone special, someone loved, and then being laughed at for what seemed like no reason at all. Because I didn't like myself very much, I found it hard to stand up to people. When she hit me, all I could think of was that my dad does worse than that and I had been hit harder before, for no reason whatsoever.

When I got home, I went to my room, took out the satanic bible and found a passage to be read for revenge. It was in another language but I sounded it out carefully. Months later, around the same time I had read the passage, I heard that the guys who had been instrumental in setting up the stunt had run into a cement barricade and smashed up their car and their heads. It was the spookiest thing I had ever experienced and it scared me straight for quite a while.

This incident was the closest thing to a spirituality that I had ever experienced up to that point in my life. It actually made me think about going back to church, to perhaps want to believe in God and heaven. I figured this was clear evidence there was some kind of higher power and, if so, I really wanted to be on the good side of God and his angels.

As for the girl in the stunt, a while later, my brother was above her standing on a wheelchair ramp that connected the first and second floors of the high school, when he spat a big hunk of phlegm onto her head and into her long hair. I have never been one to seek revenge or the kind of person who lets hate eat away at them. I think, if I had the chance, I would have made up with any of them, including the young woman. My life philosophy has left me open to a lot of attacks over the years but, at that age, I stood by it. Gandhi was my hero back then, not Clint Eastwood.

During that extra long summer of 1988, I woke up early one day to go to the West Edmonton mall. I had a bit of money but it wasn't spending money because I needed it for gas, a change float at work, lunch and other things. When I got to the mall, though, a shiny item caught my eye. It was a tiny 1.5-inch television that you could fold up and put in your pocket. It seemed like the perfect gadget for me, with all the driving around I did and the frequent long stretches of time I sometimes had to kill. It cost $100 and, even though I couldn't afford it, I decided to get it, telling myself I would work extra shifts that week and make the money back in a couple of days.

It was a long drive to the pizza restaurant I worked at. Despite the fact that my dad had warned me about using it due to the high truck traffic, I took a freeway called the Yellowhead across town. It had a higher speed limit and fewer lights than other routes and I was running late, so I didn't have a lot of choice. I wasn't far from my off-ramp when I approached a traffic light that had a truck just leaving the middle lane on a fresh green light. I signaled and changed lanes to the right of the truck and went to pass him. He built up speed fairly quickly so when I was beside him I wasn't moving past him very fast. Then, it happened.

Through The Withering Storm

I was only partially past him when I looked over to see that he was signaling to move into my lane. He couldn't see me and I was in the curb lane with nowhere to go. I don't know if slamming on my brakes would have helped, but I decided to do the opposite and floor the gas pedal on my gargantuan green car, putting all eight cylinders into action. I went as fast as I could, and by the time I was in his view but not yet past him, I was doing more than 100 km/h and my right hand wheels were just fractions of an inch from the curb. I looked up and all I could do was try and hold tight while this monster machine ground its front right wheel into my poor old Dodge.

After he scraped along my rear quarter panel for about a second, the trucker realized something was in his way and pulled back into his lane. I followed in behind him although he didn't seem to want to stop. As a caution I made note of his license plate number, but after he took an off-ramp (coincidentally the one I was headed for), he pulled over, stopped and got out.

At first, I didn't really know what to do. He tried to tell me the accident was the fault of the driver of the truck ahead of him, who had told him the lane was free. I called "bullshit" on that line and ran it down for him. I basically told him either he paid me $100 for the damage (which was actually just a bunch of bumps on an already half-rusted quarter panel) or I would call the police. He grudgingly gave in, peeled off a few $20s for me and got back in his truck. All I was thinking at the time was that it would be a good way to pay for my TV and I had got the money. I felt proud that I had stood up to the guy but, in reality, I could have gotten another car out of the whole mess, if I had been smart.

Not many people can say they were hit by an 18-wheeler and survived it. Telling the story to some people, including my parents, I was honestly surprised when they showed compassion and even shock that I had been in an accident. I had no idea that anyone cared if I lived or died. I remember telling my dad that and he got angry with me.

Unfortunately, every time anything happened, bad or good, my dad's reaction was to get angry. I often thought it was his only emotion. But, sometimes, I could see through it and tell that he was trying to show care and compassion in the only way he could. My dad had been born during the Great Depression. He was mostly raised during World War Two in occupied Denmark. When he finished grade six, he was signed up into a non-paying apprenticeship that he didn't choose and, when he had done that, he was drafted into the military. After trying unsuccessfully to save some money, he started right from scratch, crossed the planet to a place he had never been, with a language he didn't speak and ended up doing quite well. But all those years of deprivation and desperation made him hard and bitter but there was no doubt he loved his wife and his kids.

Earlier that summer, we took one of our last family trips to the arid Drumheller Valley where my uncle Joe lived. When I was a kid, uncle Joe had treated me like gold and I was really looking forward to visiting him and his wife Ernestine, who was a very sweet woman he had married after my aunt Martha passed away. I had it in mind to do some hiking and camping in the valley as well, so I brought along a backpack, tent and sleeping bag.

The night before we left, I had stayed up all night with my friend Lurch, talking, drinking coffee and playing board games. It was something of a ritual for us, although, on this occasion it was to be the last time I would see Lurch or any of my friends until the summer ended. We would meet up and go down into the basement, shoot my pellet guns, drink coffee and talk and talk and talk. He had been a bit of an expert in the occult and had me pretty worried about some of the stuff I had been doing, like using self-meditation to try and leave my body, and reading the satanic bible. He told me that if you leave your body you can become possessed and soon after your body will die. He seemed so serious about the whole thing that I got a little freaked out.

    Many years later, I found out why Lurch and I connected so well and were such good friends. The fact was that we both had a pretty distorted world view and his situation was not helped by drugs he had taken sometime after our friendship. Lurch was a paranoid schizophrenic, also untreated, and so we had a bond we couldn't explain or begin to understand until we both were under proper care for our problems. In the morning, after we had spent yet another entire night drinking coffee and talking over endless cups of strong coffee, my parents had a hard time motivating me out of the house and I slept in our van the whole way down to Drumheller.

    When we got there, my uncle was his same old lovable self to everyone but me. He constantly complained and got angry with teenagers about their behavior, which to me didn't seem fair. I can totally see now where he was coming from but, back then, I felt awful about the whole thing. This experience served to further cement my melancholy disposition and self-loathing that left me constantly asking the question of what had I done wrong, what was wrong with me, and why did people hate me so much. I still loved him dearly, though. He was like a 70 year-old kid. He had never lost his youthful innocence and sense of fun. All his life, uncle Joe had been a heavy equipment operator and I just knew this was an excuse for him to play in the dirt all day with big machines.

On the second night there, I packed up my backpack and headed out into the badlands. I hiked for a long time, then climbed to the top of a butte and set up camp on top. During the night, I had a horrible dream that my dad had died, and I woke up thinking I was home. It was such a realistic, terrifying dream that I wanted to go into my parent's room to talk to dad, but there I was, miles from civilization. It took a while, but I got back to sleep, woke up, packed my tent and camping stuff and went off to see more of the badlands.

Although I thought I was in the middle of nowhere, after hiking a few miles, something appeared to grow in the distance. When I got in close enough to see it, I thought I had lost my mind, but in fact it was one of the strangest coincidences of my life. As I walked up over a hill, there was a statue of Jesus with his arms stretched out, inviting sinners into his presence. After a little more hiking, I discovered that I had come across a place called Dinosaur National Park, and Jesus was among the statues on top of a hill, just like a similar statue in the city of Rio de Janeiro, Brazil. It may or may not have been a divine revelation, but it was enough to plant a seed in my heart. Not one that would grow soon, but a seed nonetheless.

Later that day I got back to my uncle's house, had supper and didn't share my spiritual revelations with anyone. I told the story, but left out the feeling I had that it was more than just an ordinary coincidence, or the fact that I had been experimenting with the occult and, thus, was more vulnerable to such signs.

On one of our sightseeing drives around the area, we got to see a movie being filmed. It was a

Through The Withering Storm

Canadian production about the war called *Bye Bye Blues*. I soaked up everything I saw that day. I had been fascinated with everything about movies since I was five when my parents took me to see Star Wars. For a while, my brother and I had plans and ideas on how to make our own movies. We tried to learn everything we could about special effects and cameras. My brother's interest died off and, for a while, so did mine. But, many years later, I tried to get work in movies as an extra and, eventually, worked on a few sets of local productions. It all had stemmed from walking around that small town, talking with movie people and just being enraptured by these things that I had, at that point, only seen on the screen.

Bye Bye Blues ended up being one of the better movies to come out of Canada in the past 20 years and seeing part of it being filmed was a life-changing event, perhaps even as much as "seeing Jesus."

When that summer ended, I was a whole lot happier than I had been. At that point, I was around other people my age and learning things that would earn me a future, respect and, hopefully, all of the other things I didn't have throughout that terrible, lonely summer.

Unfortunately, in the very near future, things would happen that would cause me to grow up quickly and accept the loner's life as a sad reality that would, perhaps, never go away. I was right in the worst way. There was something wrong with me and the things my illness made me do drove an even bigger wedge between myself and the people around me, including my own family. It was wedge that would prove impossible to remove without help.

Chapter Five: Fighting to Find Normal

My grade 12 year should have been the time of my life; a time for first loves, sports glory and reveling in friendships as solid as a rock. In some ways, I was having the time of my life. I had a car, nice clothes and was starting to like going to school once again. Sadly, though, it was still a time in which I often walked around in a fog of depression, constantly questioning my own worth as a human being. I still would stay up until the early hours of the morning on school nights, sometimes drinking alone, trying to settle the fires in my mind that threatened to make me self-destruct.

Friendships came and went, and I could never understand why people didn't seem to like me for more than a short time. I did know that I most often went against the grain. I had become compulsive about my hair, frequently sitting for hours over a newspaper cutting each hair with a pair of scissors down to one finger-length. I would sometimes sit in front of the TV measuring every hair and the ones I deemed too long I would cut. This was not a time when short hair was popular and I didn't have the excuse of being in cadets. This hair obsession really made me look like some kind of weirdo and, inside my mind, there were even more strange things going on. I suffered from terrible insomnia and would often stay up until an hour before school.

Then, if I was able to go, I would end up in a fog of fatigue, not eating any breakfast and almost never having done any homework. My mom had told me stories about similar things that happened to her when she was younger, but, strangely, I never saw these things in a negative light. I had no one really to talk to about my problems, so they simply compounded over time.

    As I was growing up, my mom had dealt with a lot of mental health issues herself. I remember one day coming home to find an ambulance in our backyard, not understanding why my mom kept trying to kill herself if she loved us kids so much or why she kept having to go in hospital psychiatric wards. Most of the time, she seemed so strong and so intelligent. She had read nearly 700 classic books and had come very close to going to university on a full scholarship back in the 1960's but then, in a fit of depression that coincided with some awful family problems, she tried to kill herself and ended up staying in a hospital that sounded like it existed in the dark ages. She told me stories of violence, sexual abuse, people being dragged screaming and crying – not wanting more shock treatments. And that was only the first time. She was to have many such visits to places for treatment, some better, some worse. Perhaps, it was some of those stories that made me want to deny any kind of problems of my own life, until they got so bad that almost nothing could be done.

    For me, Grade 12 was a time when I knew a lot of people and had some friends, but rarely made a connection with anyone unless there was alcohol involved. I can remember going to one guy's house where there were people I knew from grade 10, and I drank six beers in rapid succession. For some reason, I didn't just get drunk, I got quite hyper and showed some extremely poor judgment in the things I said and did. My host became really angry with me, though he didn't show it. He just banned me from ever darkening his party again.

I had no friends who really shared my interests, which were pretty much confined to literature and late night TV. Later in my grade 12 year, I reconnected with Lurch who had been homeless on the streets of Edmonton since early summer and was now living in a shelter. He was a great friend and, although there was loyalty and respect between us, there was not a lot of common interest or brotherly love. We liked to shoot, to play video games and we could keep each other up all night telling war stories, but that was about it.

It took so much to shake me out of bed in the morning that I began a vicious cycle. Because of drinking so much coffee, I was always too wired when I got home from work to sleep, so I would lose myself in old shows from the '50s that our local station played all night. A thousand times, I would sit in front of the TV and swear to myself I wouldn't waste my life in front of the idiot box but I would never get to the point of shutting it off and picking up a book, much less my school books. Although I felt better about myself and likely even started to look better, I don't think I even came close to having a date more than once or twice.

There were a lot of factors contributing to my loneliness. My alcoholism often came with a sort of manic state where I would become boisterous and even abusive and, conversely, a great deal of my time was spent in a fog of depression. I suppose family issues such as the constant fighting with my father and being indoctrinated into communism with a lot of false promises and lies from my sister's boyfriend (not to mention that he could always justify playing head games with people whenever he decided he didn't like how they thought or acted). Any of those things could have been factors as well. Lack of ready cash and

Through The Withering Storm

long hours of work also contributed to my loneliness.

It never occurred to me, even after spending years visiting my mom at hospital psychiatric wards, that I could have a genetic illness. The easy excuse was that I

was lonely because I hated myself, because I had a desire to punish myself, and that I believed I never deserved any good things in life. That was all true, of course, but I suspect that, if I could have found a way to ask for help, my problems might have been much less complex.

School got off to a great start. When I went in to register and pay my fees, I ran into an old friend who I had first gotten to know at Blue Lake. His name was Lee and the world was his oyster. He was French, and seemed to have the knack of meeting women and getting them into bed. This ability of his didn't help me at all, but often we had good times together, getting roaring drunk and talking about the constant bombardment of good and evil in our lives. We often carried out all-night drinking sessions and he was a fairly smart guy. He made his living as a DJ and was pretty good at it. I really felt lucky to have him as a friend but I was often reminded that he saw me as some kind of charity case.

Not long after we started school, through the influence of an uncle of his, Lee got a job in Quebec working with dangerous PCB chemicals (then used in electrical transformers), sending them over to Europe to be carefully disassembled and recycled. I didn't see him again for many months. I think Lee understood more about me than I did of myself. He tried hard to get me to do fun things such as throwing the football around, which I really used to like but gave up in elementary school. We would also play racquetball or charm waitresses into not asking us for ID to prove we were old enough to drink. It was just cool to have such a friend, but unfortunately it didn't last. While he was away, we didn't speak at all.

Although I was supposed to be catching up with my math courses and taking Math 10 that year, I opted to take it by correspondence (which I never got finished) and, in place of it, I took Law 12 and English 12 instead. By a stroke of luck, my old friend Will, with whom I had parted company over something minor some time ago, was in my law class. Will and I became friends again and had quite a good time in Law 12.

I actually took a great interest in that law class, because, at the time, I had hopes and dreams of becoming a lawyer. Armed with the left-wing rhetoric of my sister's boyfriend, I got to practice my debating skills in that class quite a bit. I thought that somehow espousing views of a differing political system, and how it was better than the Canadian or American system, would win me respect. I must have been seen as the weirdest kid in school, despite the fact that I displayed intelligence that often surpassed even that of my teacher.

Each day, I would talk to my sister's boyfriend on the phone or in person, and each day my teacher would watch Oprah. The next day we would go in and bash heads together. He was a terribly nice guy but I think he hated me. He was one of those teachers who would rather make friends with his students than cater to the shining stars in his classes. He and a couple of other teachers went into a bar and found some of their underage students drinking. Instead of turning them in, they bought the students a round and left. Friendship was more important than respect.

Through The Withering Storm

When the course ended, we had a two-part final and I wrote the first part. Then, the unthinkable happened. Due to my insomnia, I slept in for the second half of the exam, and missed it completely. Up to that point, I had close to a 90 per cent average. After the exam was counted as zero, it went down to the low 60s. I was devastated. If it had not been for all the disagreeing and arguing and leaving class early, I think my teacher might have let me re-write the test. Instead, he was left smirking and I had a permanent black mark on my record.

In English 12, I worked very hard and greatly respected my teacher. I wanted to be a lawyer and planned on taking psychology as my undergraduate degree. (I have often heard that many psychology students are in fact taking those courses to find out what is wrong with them.) But, I always knew that, deep inside of me, lurked a writer wanting to get out. And though I hated some parts of it, I knew I would need a superior command of the English language to succeed in anything I chose to do. That year, in English, our teacher took us through Shakespeare's Hamlet, which had me captivated because it was the story of a young Dane with a black and dreary disposition, pretty much like me, aside from a few small details.

Near the beginning of the school year, I had decided that my pizza job wasn't enough, so I went to my sister's boyfriend, George, and got him to agree to train me as a donut baker. At the same time, my dad (who was a sign writer) got a contract to put lettering on the doors on all the stairwells in a huge new federal government building in downtown Edmonton and he needed some help. I would get off school Friday, sleep a couple of hours, deliver pizza all evening, then head for the donut shop and try to learn something.

When that was done, I would work all Saturday for my dad. I don't know what kept me going through those days. I was a mental and physical wreck and had no social life at all. After a while, I gave up on the donut idea, and my dad and I finished the contract with the government. All that was left was the pizza job.

Although it was a fun job and I got to eat out a lot, I hated working in Edmonton, never seeing the same person twice, not working with any of my friends. I wanted out and I didn't know how to do it, so one day I simply dropped off an order and drove home in the middle of a shift. I was like that. I guess I'm still like that. When I hit a roadblock, like I did when I suddenly realized my job was getting me nowhere, I would just throw in the towel, move on, and never look back. I never even saw the point of finishing the day out. I just took off. It was an incredible feeling of freedom sometimes to do that, because no one could really own me. A lot of people in this society feel if they have a few more dollars than someone who works for them, they can treat them badly and they have to take it. I didn't, and still don't, believe in that concept. This attitude caused me great amounts of pain and hardship in years to come.

When I got home from Edmonton, after ditching the pizza job, I called my boss and told him my brakes had gone and never went back to work for him. Soon after, I got a better paying pizza job in St. Albert, at a place that was run by a generous and kindly Egyptian who I used to sit with and talk for hours and hours. Mostly we talked about business and, in a way, he became something of a father figure to me. He let me know that my most important goal in life was to be a gentleman and deal honestly with people. He was a great boss and made a pretty mean pizza as well.

One of our biggest assignments in English 30 was a project where we had to go out and find two works of an author, read them, write a thesis statement about them, then write a mini 'thesis' on our statement. Although I was arguing tooth and nail at the time with my law teacher, maintaining my left wing viewpoints, I picked one of the more right-wing authors in modern times, Rudyard Kipling. I had become fascinated with his poem "If" which stated: "If you can wait and not be tired from waiting…." The poem was supposedly an ode to his son and I loved every word of it from the very first time I heard it. Also, one of my favorite movies of all time was a Michael Caine/Sean Connery film called *The Man Who Would Be King*, which was based on a story by Kipling.

I took these two works and compared and contrasted them. The only problem was that I had been given five months to do this and I let it sit for four months and 28 days. When I look back now at how I lived then, staying up all night, working shift work and filling my body with pizza and hamburgers, and neglecting the one thing I was any good at (school), it hardly seems sane. That was how my actions and life choices were decided for me – not only by my job and family but also by some strange force inside me that was slowly eating away at my psyche.

By some stroke of luck, I squeezed out 70 per cent on my thesis but I was still headed for academic disaster. There was really no way I was going to make it to university without taking a second and maybe even a third year of grade 12 and I knew my home life wouldn't allow me to do that. My dad had made it clear that once I reached my 18th birthday, I had better find another place to live. Sometimes, he would get so angry with me he didn't even want to wait the few months until that time. Sometimes, screaming and even crying, I would yell back and tell him that he was responsible for me until I turned 18. I don't think that was exactly true, but I had to hold on to something.

I didn't know any other home but our townhouse in St. Albert and I had no idea on how to rent an apartment. I kept denying that there was anything wrong and kept staying up all night watching TV, smoking cigarettes or cigars until the wee hours of the morning. I just couldn't accept the reality that I was alone in the world. My parents didn't want me, I had no prospects for a roommate, and I had no one who would take me in. A few years back, Lurch had run away. He contacted me and showed me around to where he and his friends lived. It was appalling. Apartments without power, rotting walls, filled with street people with no morals or consideration. Despite that I worked, made good money, had a car and got good grades, if and when my dad succeeded in kicking me out of the house, I had little doubt I would end up homeless or living in a garbage bin or parking garage within a short time.

When the time came for classes to start up again after the first-semester exams, I went to the pool hall with Will during a class break, spending some time reflecting on what was happening and what I was going to do. I knew I had to get serious; I had to take a full course load and do well on all my courses. I was set up for chemistry, physics and social studies, all at the grade 12 levels. Within a week I discovered that Math 10, which I had dropped, and not yet made up in correspondence, was a pre-requisite for grade 12 physics and I had no hope of passing the course without it. So I dropped physics and left myself with a bare minimum of involvement in school, just two courses, chemistry and social studies. I didn't go to dances, I didn't join any committees, I just went to my two classes and left. Lee had come back into town and, when I wasn't working weekends, we would often get together.

We got deliriously drunk weekend after weekend and, as time went on, I was having more difficulty accepting my own behavior with alcohol while I dealt with the difficult consequences of growing up with an alcoholic father. It was not until years later that I started to see myself turning into the kind of drinker my dad was. I thought I was safe because I didn't drink alone. When I drank alone, I thought I was safe because I didn't drink every day. It was a problem that was heading toward me like a runaway train.

It seems that all I did was oppose people that year. I would get into fights with my dad, I would argue God versus my impressions of the spiritual with Lee, I would argue communism against capitalism in school. I ended up feeling outcast and alone, but somehow I dragged myself through to the end of grade 12. We had a graduation ceremony but I didn't go since I didn't have enough credits to graduate.

When I look back, I see that as being more of a blow to my mom than a defeat for me. When I was younger, she had said that the proudest day of her life would be when she watched me graduate high school. She felt that way because she had nearly finished high school and had done very well. She was right on the verge of a full scholarship to become a teacher and, as a result of some severe family problems; she had a mental collapse and tried to kill herself. Sometimes, when she felt up to it, she would talk about the horrors in the hospital, the shock treatments and high doses of tranquilizers. In the end, I learned more about those places than I ever wanted to know.

Although I didn't graduate, I couldn't wait to go to an after-grad party that was held on the nearby airbase. We were taken out and brought back on busses and everyone was there, most of them with an assortment of booze or drugs. We were also provided with a cord of wood to make a huge fire and a DJ with concert speakers to blast us into our new lives in style.

I can't get over how influential that night was and how much went on. I ran into one of my old Air Cadet friends there, a guy who later was to pilot the CF-18 Hornet fighter jet and nearly had a job with NASA. I also talked to the DJ and requested a song he didn't have, but I kept requesting it until he nearly punched me. I got away with it because he was also an old cadet friend. His girlfriend Tracy (the very first girl I ever danced with at a cadet dance) was there, and I tried telling her about how she was always such a nice person and how I was sad that I wouldn't see her again, when she grabbed me and stuck her tongue down my throat right in front of her boyfriend – a full French kiss. I don't know why but it didn't seem to faze her boyfriend. Still, I wasn't going to fully escape getting a beating that night.

After Tracy kissed me, I felt pretty much indestructible. I walked through a crowd of people who were dancing and I kept getting knocked, pushed and shoved. I thought they were slam dancing so I started pushing and slamming back, but then some little jerk started punching me in the face. I didn't fight back, just let him hit me until some big jock held him back and another big jock nearly pushed me off my feet and told me to go away. I had nothing against

Through The Withering Storm

the little jerk but I had a strong inclination to punch out the jock that pushed me. Still, I walked off and sat down at the fire near a girl I had known from school and work.

I remember feeling pretty horrible at that point. Here was the old curse come back to haunt me, the curse that dictated there was no way in the world I was ever going to have a good time long enough to feel good about myself. Still, I decided to chat with my old friend Jessica. The fire was now starting to dwindle, and I could barely make out her date, though I could see he was a bit dark-skinned.

The guy I could barely see turned out to be an ex-Sea cadet and we shared an interest in cigars. I was very drunk and could barely hold a conversation. For some reason, he took down my number and not long after he called me up and I decided to meet up with him. In no time at all, we were best friends, close as brothers. He ended up joining the military full time and I saw him often, even spent time on the base with him in Calgary. It was a strange kind of friendship, though. In many ways we were different but, above all, we respected each other. However, over the years a lot changed with both of us, and yet another friend I had really hoped to have for a long time was out of my life permanently.

After the party, when the sun finally started coming up, I got into one of the vans that were there to take us home and prevent us from driving home drunk. In my particular van, a minor league hockey player who I had become friends with in Chemistry 12, his girlfriend, and a friend of mine named Dan, all rode back to St. Albert together. I convinced Dan to come with me to my place so we could get my car and go play some pool in Edmonton. Dan liked the idea, and when the van let us off I took out my keys and tried in vain to fit the key to the lock of my car. Then I looked up and there was the van, blocking my exit. "Oh shit!" I exclaimed, and promised them I was only kidding and that I would throw my keys in the house and just go for a walk to sober up. When the van left, for some reason there were three of us. Somehow a schoolmate named Frank had shown up in my back yard and we had no idea how.

Frank was even drunker than we were (and we could barely stand straight), so we locked him in the garden shed and went out walking. On our way, we held up a paperboy for just one paper, so we could read the comics, then we went into a schoolyard and I started kicking a wall and saying, "What are you trying to teach us!" I then heard Dan say the same thing but also heard a bunch of glass smashing. Looking over, I could see he had kicked out a window. Dan had always seemed such a gentle, nerdy kind of guy I didn't think he was capable of such vandalism.

Dan was the kind of guy who had likely been pushed around as much in school as I had, but he was a hard-core drinker. When you take all the pain and abuse of a young lifetime, mix it in with your final goodbye to the friends you grew up with, then blend it all with a lot of drinking, you have enough to pop the lid off just about anyone. I think that was what happened with Dan. But smashing that window wasn't even enough for his supposed-adult mind. To top things off, he got his hands on some kid's bike and, moving very wobbly and shakily, rode it towards his house which was three miles away, up a river valley. I was too drunk to protest so I headed back home.

When I got there, I went downstairs to get my keys and go to bed, but things didn't look quite right.

Through The Withering Storm

There were three piles of laundry where before there had been only two. Then I realized the third pile was actually Frank, curled up in the fetal position on my basement floor. I threw him out and went to bed. Eight or 10 hours later I woke up and there was a mess in the bathroom. Apparently, my dad had run into Frank in the yard, had set him up in the spare bedroom, and later came up and found him sleeping on the floor of the bathroom with his pants down and crap all over the place. I went back to sleep for a while, then we gave "Mr. Poopie" a ride home. In three or four days my hangover was gone, but even now Frank's friends haven't let him forget that night.

Near the end of my grade 12 year, I got a job working in a plastics assembly plant and soon discovered where writers had been inspired by ideas of hell. Eight solid hours of endless noise. Every five seconds another plastic pail to either put a cap on, or a handle on, or a lid on. On and on and on. I had the job for two weeks and they offered to hire me on full time. I wanted to tell them precisely where they could stuff that idea, but just said I needed to finish school, and that it was a promise I had made to my mother.

I left there with a check for $570, took it to the bank and asked for a $400 deposit, five 20s and 70 one-dollar bills. I walked around feeling like a real hot shot with a huge roll of money. Not long after, I was driving through Edmonton with my friend Will from law class in and I spotted the coolest looking car I had ever seen. Not thinking I could afford it, Will and I drove up to this beautiful pearl white 1978 Ford Cobra that was on sale for $1,000. I don't know how I managed it but I talked my dad into helping me get a loan. Before I knew it the Cobra was mine and I was blasting through the streets in style. A day or two after I bought the car, I asked a friend which car he would want if he could have any in the student parking lot (and this was a wealthy suburban school). He looked around for a while and finally said, "Oh, that Cobra over there." I dangled the keys and even let him drive it a bit. The main problem with that car, though, was that I was a death-defying idiot who thought I could impress people with speed, stunts and a loud stereo. The reality was that, inside that beautiful car, was a tortured and lonely young man trying to make a connection using a burned out fuse.

That spring I was good friends with a fellow named Keith, who managed to get me a double date with a girl that had come up from the U.S. to live with her uncle, a pastor who was supposed to turn her life around. Her name was Charlene and she was a very sad case. She was good looking enough, but soon after meeting her I could tell she had a lot of problems. Keith, his girlfriend, Charlene, and I went out cruising in my car, went to my favorite pool hall, for a walk downtown, hit all the popular parts of Edmonton, then decided to go back to St. Albert to watch a movie at Keith's house.

We got there and, within a few minutes, Charlene and I were necking. We went downstairs and tried to have sex but nothing felt right. I was out of shape and over-tired and we couldn't go through with the act. To add insult to injury, the next day my skin had broken out in a rash all over my face, most likely because of how nervous I was. I felt like I was attractive enough, like I was a normal teenager with a normal life but that only lasted two days.

Charlene seemed to like me and I couldn't understand why. That same night I took her to visit a friend who worked in an all-night gas station, and just left her there. I parked my car in a deserted spot in a mall parking lot and nearly started crying. I couldn't let myself be weak. I couldn't let myself be loved. My self-loathing and depression ran too deep. I knew I was off the deep end, but didn't use it as a reason to get help; I used it as a reason to push others away. I even composed and whispered a speech I would tell Charlene to explain why I couldn't be her boyfriend. It went something like: "I'm an alcoholic, suicidal, manic depressive with barely any money." It turned out I wasn't going to get a chance to use my speech anyway because even the brief feeling of joy I had thinking Charlene liked me, went away.

    I found out from my friend that she was in fact a hooker and had been turning tricks and probably had done so for a while. I felt like I needed an HIV test and that I was just another piece of scum. I said goodbye to my childhood and slowly started to realize that I was barely prepared for the outside world that was now looming over me like a thundercloud.

    After my last exam that year, I went to work for just a couple of days with the same pizza place where I had cooked for a year before, this time delivering. The money was great but I really didn't like the idea of a company just wanting me for my precious Cobra, which was still a used car and wouldn't last very long. I also didn't like the idea that I would be behind the wheel so much that I would get sick of driving and the one thing I spent the most on in my life — my car, would be mostly a burden to me. So, I went to a student placement agency and ended up finding a job at a gas station in St. Albert.

    The pay wasn't that great but there was a fair bit of free time to be had in between cars and there were some pretty cool guys working there. It was the first time I spent a good deal of time with cool people and at first I didn't really know how to act but, after a while I began to really like it.

During the day, I would work and during the night I would spend a lot of time at local pool halls, rarely playing anyone but constantly practicing. I drove away a lot of possible friends with my political views that by now were as far left of centre as they would ever go. I prattled on about the prime minister of Canada, about American president George Bush, about the upper class and how their media and corporate policy kept us under their heel. I don't know why but I thought I could be a force for change, like Castro and his brave liberation of Cuba from the American military industrial complex. I tried to rationalize everything, hating the rich but living in Canada's fifth richest community. I wanted to change the world but simply passed time arguing with people who either didn't care or would always remain opposed to me.

Each day, I would work three to eight hours, play some pool somewhere or hang out at the corner store on my block, then come home and stay up until my parents went to bed. Then, I would make a pot of tea and sit at the kitchen table reading far into the night. I started out with a book my sister's boyfriend said that I simply had to read called Les Misérables by Victor Hugo. I got a lot out of it as it talked at length about love, giving and sacrifice, things I thought I understood but never quite looked at in that way before. I think it took me three weeks to read the book. My main complaint about "Les Misérables" was that half of it was in French and I had a very limited understanding of the language.

That summer I also read some Farley Mowat and Mordecai Richler, Canadian authors, and a couple of Shakespearean plays. I was trying my hardest to grow up in a hurry and prepare for university. I would even read the news at work although I knew little

Through The Withering Storm

about Israel and Iran or pretty much any place in the Middle East, from where a lot of the news was coming at that time. There was trouble stirring in the Persian Gulf and soon it would hit close to home, not least of all because one of my workmates was from Kuwait.

All in all, that summer was a good one for me. One development that stood out was that I started losing my acne, got a great tan from work and was finally starting to see myself as attractive. I had no experience in speaking with the opposite sex but the whole idea seemed less impossible now.

The worst part of that summer was that every night, when work or play was over and it was time to drive home, I fell into a deep cloud of depression; a foul, black mood that swept over me like a storm. And, to top it off, I always had to lie in bed quietly for hours before falling asleep. I honestly thought these things were normal, so I never talked to anyone about them. I just kept getting worse and worse. I remember a deep feeling of drifting away from who I had wanted to be.

At the same time, I began to have a strong sense that my youth was slipping away, and so, at the last possible moment, I decided my best course of action was to once again register for school. That may have been the worst mistake of my life ... up until then.

I can remember the ending of that summer as clear as though it were etched on the wall of my living room. A mural to constantly remind me that I tried too hard to hold onto my youth, and, in the process, let it slip even farther away. I made the decision to go back to school without consulting my parents and signed up for Chemistry 12, Math 10 and French 10. The math and French courses were required for university, which meant if I ever wanted to earn more than the $4.75 an hour I was getting back then, I had to take them and pass them, regardless of the fact they were grade 10 courses being taken by a once-failed grade 12 student or not. The added motivation for French 10 was that I felt like a fool reading Les Misérables in the summer and not understanding half of it, especially since I was of French heritage on my mother's side. This course was destined to teach me a lot and ended up having a big impact on what was to transpire in the next few years of my life.

On my first day of French class, I picked the best seat, put my feet up and refuse to let anyone take the seat in front of me so I would have a footstool all semester. After a few people tried and failed to get the seat, a highly attractive reddish-brown haired young woman walked in, looked at me and smiled, came to the back of the room and sat down next to me. She was radiant and gorgeous and I think it was love at first sight.

I became friends with her over the next while and she really came to be something special to me. We talked nearly every day and I found out she was from Calgary, which meant that for the time being at least, she was single. Her name was Wendy, the kind of name that rolled off a person's tongue with images of romance and the sweet sensation of love and happiness, or at least that was what it did for me at the time.

Chemistry and math were standard courses but I decided to try really hard to do well with all three subjects. The main problem was that pressure at home was starting to increase. In my dad's house, attendance at the dinner table was mandatory every night I was home. Yet every night I sat down with my dad, we would get into screaming arguments that

Through The Withering Storm

often ended with blows. I tried my best to stay out of his way but I was just as bull-headed as he was on some issues, even resorting to insults laced with profanity. All the while my mom just looked on, helpless to do anything. Work was going okay but not long after I started back at school a bunch of people that I used to know in grade 11 came by the gas station. They stopped at the pumps and one by one, each with a somber look, got out and stood in front of me silently.

"Glen's dead," one of them said. Glen, my good friend, the guy who even right up to a couple of weeks before was the super-glue that held me together with these people, the guy who was always there to talk with, always there to count on. They told me it was suicide. I walked inside the gas station, told the other employee that I was leaving early and then walked with them to the liquor store and bought a Mickey. I wanted to get drunk and get drunk fast. I wanted to lash out at the society that allowed people to end up feeling so useless and unwanted that they ended up this way. I wanted to die myself.

I had never experienced the death of someone so close to me. I was still only 17; in the eyes of the law, a child. We all went to a house and drank and drank. I found out that Glen's girlfriend had left him for one of his best friends and he ended up acting strangely and staying outside this girl's door all night. He then went to the home of another friend who was a hunter, took a gun and shot himself while his hunter friend was out.

What really got to me was that no one seemed to care. My teachers, Glen's former teachers, my boss, customers at the gas station who knew Glen. They all just smiled and shook it off. I was devastated. I never saw his death as his revenge on the girlfriend who betrayed him, but more as one last sad act from a mentally ill young person with the entire world ahead of him.

I also saw his death as a mirror to my own feelings. On the outside, I had a job, a nice family and did well in school. On the inside, I was living in a personal hell and losing a part of myself a little at a time, with each fight with my dad, with each argument where everyone thought I was crazy. Though I never wanted to take the final step that Glen did, I wasn't as far off from it as I would have liked to think. A lot of my behavior, especially in the way I drove my car, blasting through lights, racing, stunting, flying around corners, unable to see what could have been coming, was verging on suicidal.

But aside from drinking a lot and being angry for a while, I kept it all inside, never talked to anyone. Out of disgust for the teachers who made a big deal out of giving me mourning and funeral time off, I dropped chemistry and math and just kept going with French. I didn't know what else to do. School was my anchor and that one course was the only thing that mattered to me anymore.

Time passed slowly and one night the fellow I was working with forgot to shut down the gas pumps when we closed so $30,000 worth of gas was left sitting all night free for the taking. We were both fired so I filed a grievance with the labor board. In the U.S. at the time, when you were wrongly fired, you could sue, but all I could do was claim that my boss hadn't given me enough notice of termination. I spent the next six months fighting him over about $130. On the brighter side, within a week I went to a giant grocery store in Edmonton and got a job for $3.25 an hour more than the gas station paid to work the night shift stocking shelves. It was a long drive

Through The Withering Storm

but the job got me in shape. It was a good working environment. The company allowed music over the PA system for us at night and generally we would only work a four-hour shift then head home after going for coffee somewhere close.

It was around that time that I started to associate with more people but not necessarily morally strong people. One of them was a human sponge I only want to call PGS. He was a 21-year-old computer nerd who never held down a normal job for long and who was stuck on a young girl of 14 on whom he was constantly cheating. One night, he would call up and want a ride to her group home. Another night, he would be with her and want me to drive him to the lake so he could break into his parent's trailer. PGS knew the night people at 7-Eleven and talked them into giving him free cigarettes, which soon became his only form of currency. I got to be friends with one of the night people and had also known the assistant manager from my cadet days. Pretty soon I wasn't paying for anything either. It was an incredibly easy trap to fall into.

Christmas that year was pretty much the end of life as I knew it and the beginning of what was to become an adulthood that was far from the happy times and the love of a close family as it could ever be. I was about to face eons of loneliness and pain and running from the demons within me for many years to come. As for my home life at that point though, pressure was increasing daily, and it was starting to show to the people at school and to my mom and sister. I even went to one of my teachers and tried to explain what a horrible situation I was in never knowing if I would even have a home by the next day, constantly arguing with my dad, constantly getting into escalating fights with him. I once heard that a group of Rhesus monkeys had been tested by being shocked constantly after actions within a certain criteria and were given these punishments whether they did good or bad. As a hardworking young man, it seemed this was what was happening to me. I would work hard, make money, work hard, get good grades, and still I was going through these awful times under my dad's rule. What happened to the monkeys under this treatment? They ended up going almost completely insane, even displaying manic-depressive states of randomly going manic and alternately going into a depressive fog.

    One day, I saw Wendy drive by in an expensive car with her brother and mother while I was walking home two miles in the snow. I so desperately wanted to reach out to her, tell her I loved her and I needed her help. There seemed to be nowhere to go, nothing I could do. I thought a lot at that time about Wendy; she seemed so beautiful and happy and came from a nice family. Her father was a bank manager and she had no trouble fitting in despite moving in the last summer from Calgary. I had missed my chance with her, which to a normal teenager would have been just a small setback, but to me was the end of the world. I was in such an awful state and it seemed I was losing everything.

    Despite the fact that I was still far from finishing high school, my dad felt it was time for me to move out of the family home. He hadn't picked a specific time but on Christmas Eve, after my mom had spent hours upon hours painstakingly preparing all of our favorite Christmas dishes, from devilled eggs to raisin pie, my dad decided to lay into me. When I fought back with a tirade of my own, he cancelled Christmas for everyone. My sister and brother and my sister's

Through The Withering Storm

boyfriend had come and we were all prepared for a huge feast followed by the opening of presents. Not that year and not for many years to come.

I had never felt worse or less loved than I did at that moment. The first thing I did was drive out to Edmonton and I ended up selling my precious Ford Cobra for about half of what it was worth and tried to find an apartment close to work and the bus routes. This was a hell of a thing to try and do in Edmonton on Christmas Eve. I did end up finding one but it was a mess and I didn't rent it. Filthy cigarette-burned carpets and cracking, peeling paint everywhere. It also cost more than I could reasonably afford with the hours I was getting.

More critically, because of where the cheaper apartments were located, I would most likely have to quit school. Up to that point, I had believed that school was the most important thing in my life, that you were nothing without a high school diploma. For eight years prior, I had even prepared myself for the high costs of university by stashing away thousands of mint condition comic books that I had hoped I could sell. Now, I lacked the math credits to get into university and also needed the French course I was taking, so within a few weeks, the one thing I really loved to do – study – was going to end for me. This was a long way from first grade when testing was done that revealed a child prodigy who had the potential to do anything. Here I was, about to become a high school dropout living in a slum, schlepping boxes for a living.

I ended up doing what I had hoped not to do. I went to my dad and literally begged him to let me finish school. He caved in. We went and got another loan and I bought a Honda Civic, the same year as my Cobra.

I hadn't solved any problems and a good part of what remained of my self-esteem vanished. Despite all this, I never blamed my dad. I knew he had been through horrors from war to poverty, abuse, loneliness and alcoholism. I loved him and a big part of me was hurt when we argued.

I decided to try and make some friends, get in shape, and maybe even become a stronger person. Earlier in the school year, a friend had convinced me to take some skiing lessons and it was the most fun I had ever had. Gliding down these hills south of Edmonton, getting a thrill from the speed and the challenge of staying upright; it was even better than the feeling I had driving my Cobra. Earlier in high school, I looked down at jocks, always thought they were inferior in some way but, after learning to ski, I felt differently. I even started playing racquetball and my job had made me leaner and stronger. However, competing in school against life-long jocks was to prove to be another job altogether, on the sports field and off.

Through The Withering Storm

Chapter Six: Falling Off the Edge of Reality

My physical education class showed me I had a long way to go. The first thing we did was a fitness test and I had to run a kilometer or two on runners that I thought were a great deal at $6.99. I felt like I had broken a foot and quickly spent big bucks on a pair of fancy court shoes for about $100.

The class was really a lot of fun. We would play a different sport every two weeks and I found that if I threw myself into it the way I used to throw myself into cadet activities, I would do well. On the side, I also started running and lifting weights. It didn't take long before I was noticeably fitter and, hopefully, more noticeable to the women with whom I went to school.

My job was going well but it was getting harder and harder to maintain a full course load during the day and still put in four hours at work nearly every night. I was on a constant rollercoaster of stress, from work to school to fighting with my dad. I was going home and napping after school and having terrible nightmares.

My brain was beginning to rebel against me and I had no idea how to stop it. So many things didn't make sense to me. I could see myself falling off a cliff of mental health issues and being totally unable to slow or stop my fall. Around this time, I had a talk with my mom and told her I would like to see a psychiatrist. She offered to let me have her next appointment with her doctor but, for some reason, it never materialized. My last small cry for help went almost completely unnoticed.

LEIF GREGERSEN

Over the Christmas holidays, I had borrowed a book on speed-reading and went through it with the resolve of becoming a book sponge (which I practically was already). After a while, I had trained myself to the point where I was reading a 350-page novel nearly every day, plus fulfilling all my other responsibilities. Fortunately, work was one of the easier things I had to do. I liked a lot of the people there and we got to do a lot of silly things like blast around the store on pallet jacks using them like scooters.

During one of these times, I took a wrong turn and drove right through a freshly mopped area leaving three black lines across the pristine white tile the janitors had spent a great deal of effort on keeping clean. There was nothing I could do to make it up to them. Union rules prevented me from picking up a mop and I couldn't even apologize to them because most of them didn't speak English. I remember another time I took the plastic off a box and threw it at a guy who responded by throwing a large bag of coffee beans at my head. The bag exploded all over the floor. Again, nothing could be done unless one of the supervisors saw it, and mostly they didn't care either.

Slowly, around that time, I started to slip away from reality. I think it all started as I modeled my behavior on some of the tough guys I knew and some of the more famous bad-asses on TV. There wasn't really any specific role model but more a conglomerate of a lifetime of macho bullshit I lived around in school and my neighborhood, and the nonsense that comes out of the TV screen. I started to think that, if I followed a certain course of action proscribed for a male athlete, I could do no wrong.

Through The Withering Storm

Somehow the 'sick' part of my mind convincingly made me believe that all of my 18 years of upbringing was false. It was like being transported to another planet where all the rules were different and I had some kind of alien communication putting thoughts into my brain. I started to believe I could have any woman, take any money, beat anyone up to get what I thought I was entitled to. It was a slow transformation and I tried desperately hard to not be that kind of person but inside my mind something had cracked.

I often wondered in retrospect over the years if I didn't start to lose touch because of the murderous schedule I had set for myself. In the end, I suppose, it was genetics that really decided things but those dark days before the shit really hit the fan probably didn't help much.

It was actually while I was working at the grocery store that I had my first major meltdown. Of all things to remember, I have a clear memory of having long hair, or at least longer hair than I had for most of my life. I went into work one day, sat down at a table in the coffee room and started to carve a word in one of the tables with the edge of a spoon or something. Some guy said to me, "quit defacing the table!" I replied, "fuck off, geek!" and went on defacing the table.

After a few minutes, it was time to head downstairs and start our shift and I went with the others. I walked down like I owned the place and nearly walked into a few people who barely got out of my way. I wish I could show before and after pictures of me up to this point and me in the state I am describing. Just about anyone who knew me before then would describe me as polite to a fault but this illness totally changed me.

I got to a pallet of boxes, got a cart and started to work cutting open boxes and putting them on my cart. But after about five minutes, I just stopped, looked around, and asked myself why I was doing this. I really didn't understand at the time why I wanted to work at such a lousy time of day in a job I didn't enjoy and that caused me way too much stress. My answer? I walked right out of the store. At the front door, my boss had radioed ahead to get the security guard to stop me.

"Bernie said that I'm not to let you out until he comes to talk to you and if you leave you aren't getting back in," were the words that greeted me at the door.

"I'll tell you what." I replied, "You have no right to detain me here and if you try to I am going to kick the fucking shit out of you and leave anyway. Now open this door!"

The door opened, I walked out and turned my back on the best paying job I ever had.

It's hard to explain where these thoughts came from but I will try. All my life growing up, I had dealt with people whose parents had lots of money and tons of friends, in other words quite privileged kids. I never really understood why I felt so inferior to them and why a lot of them would pick on me. At this point, when I walked out on my job, I was deluded into believing that I could somehow live without money, play sports all the time and keep going to school. There was no analysis of details like the problems with my parents, the fact that I had, at some point, stopped eating and mostly stopped sleeping. There was just this overwhelming desire to only do the things I liked doing and let the rest of the universe somehow take care of me. I was getting bad but I wasn't yet totally non-functioning.

Through The Withering Storm

Not long after this all happened, spring break came and my sister, her boyfriend, my brother and I went up to the mountains to do a bit of cross-country skiing. This was when everyone really started to notice that something was seriously wrong with me, although they were powerless to do anything. By the end of the trip, they were all starting to wonder what had happened to me or what kind of drugs I was on.

Not long after that, a friend of mine called and asked if I wanted to go down to a left-wing charity organization in Edmonton and I agreed. When I got there, I simply stood up and walked out and started walking towards my sister's apartment, way across town and across the river valley, maybe four or kilometers, in winter. I loved my sister dearly, at this point looked up to her boyfriend for inspiration, and just wanted to go and see them. As I was walking, if I heard a horn honk I thought it was encouragement for some special mission I was on. Each time, someone looked at me or turned their car near me I thought it had some special meaning. I walked and walked, through the snow, down the valley, up the valley, and got all the way to my sister's apartment.

All the while, it was like I was outside of my body watching myself take this ridiculously long walk in the cold. I saw myself as some proud leftist soldier going to report for his final orders. Everything, it seemed, had some element of death in it. Maybe subconsciously, I understood I was horribly sick and since I didn't understand how any form of treatment could make me better, death was what must follow, by my hand or by some act of what I then thought of as bravery.

When I got to their apartment, my sister's boyfriend answered the door and said he couldn't let me in. A number of times in the past I had asked

them over the phone if I could come over and they
said no, and then I would find out that my brother had
later dropped in to see them. They told me that he had
just shown up, so here I was, just showing up. I
walked in past him and into their apartment and lay
down on their couch. My sister's boyfriend stood
over me and said "how dare you threaten my family,"
gave me a solid karate chop to the abdomen and then
picked me up and threw me out in the hall. I didn't
understand why he had done this and, since I was full
of strange ideas, I responded by taking off my clothes
and walking up and down the halls shouting protest
slogans. They called the cops and I was taken down,
beaten up some more, put in an ambulance and taken
to the hospital across the street. Again and again, they
asked me if I had done drugs, why I had done this,
why I had walked across the city and my answers
were the same. I hadn't done drugs, I had practically
never done drugs and I really didn't know why I did
all these things.

    My sister was terribly worried about me.
None of it made sense. My parents had come all the
way from out of town to the hospital and both of them
were nearly in tears. Something had happened to me
and it was obviously very serious. All my life, I had
been the example of politeness, a hard-working and
honest person and here I was saying things that didn't
make sense, off in a mental high that no one
comprehended, tied to a hospital bed with no clothes
on.

    Even now, the image of that is almost too
painful to think about. I remember them telling the
doctor they had been terribly proud of me, working so
hard, bringing home good grades, quitting smoking
and doing charity work. I felt really bad that I had let
them down but I was in a strange state. I didn't see

anything wrong with what I had done, didn't have any sense that I was losing my mind, though I was clearly out of it.

I was put on a fifth floor ward with a very old man as a roommate. That was a bit scary to me because I thought they had put me there because I was a lost cause. From when I had arrived, I was in a constant state of nausea and really felt like I was going to die. I was put through a battery of tests and had a 24-hour guard to make sure I didn't go anywhere. One of the things that really surprised me was that I had gone down to 145 lbs. when I had usually been 170 and still called skinny for most of high school. They wanted me to stay there and go through a six-month program but I kept insisting I had to finish school and finally there was nothing they could say. I was due to be released after about a week.

When it came time to be released, my dad was going to pick me up but I had delusions that told me to go home myself on the bus. As I walked out of my room, carrying the flowers in a mug my sister had brought me, I saw decorations in some places and a "teletype" voice in my head told me there was a goodbye party going on – thrown for me. It wasn't a normal or steady voice, more like ideas that had made their way into my head by crossed signals that were extremely convincing, though they made sense only to me. I got on the bus, made my way home and my parents were worried sick, not knowing where I had ended up. They took me back to the hospital, hoping this time they could convince me there was something wrong with me and I should stay but I insisted they let me go and the next day I was home.

For the next few days in school, I sat around not doing much, trying to quell rumors that I had gone batty. A good friend of mine, who had just broken up with his girlfriend, came to visit and needed some comforting. I got him in a good mood by telling him before he knew it he would have another girlfriend and succeeded in cheering him up. Then, I started going on about how I needed some drugs. This particular friend had connections but rarely used them and he knew I never used drugs so he was kind of concerned. I kept going on about this and mostly making no sense so he took me to the local hospital.

I will never forget sitting in that waiting room not knowing what was going to happen, still making my trademark corny jokes, and my friend being scared out of his wits while I thought nothing bad could happen to me. Little did I know, I was about to be introduced to the most horrible, will-breaking place on earth, a hospital for the insane.

Meanwhile at our local hospital, the same one where I was born, I got in to see a doctor. A short while later a couple of police officers came, held me down, I was injected with some vile substance that made all my muscles seize up and I was taken to what seemed like some secret location which was the mental hospital. There, I was placed in a small room locked from the outside, with no furniture and just one small window high and out of reach.

I was now officially certified. Nothing could be worse than that feeling of being drugged and locked away.

Most people would think that, at this point, one would sit down, listen to their doctor, take their medication and start down the long road to recovery. For me, however, that road was a long way off. I was full of delusions and paranoia. I would spit out medications, call my doctors names and despised some of the staff because of the way they treated me.

Through The Withering Storm

There is no end to the tricks your mind can play on you when you are sick. I can remember the staff showing us the movie *Total Recall*, where Arnold Schwarzenegger is given a memory implant. The machine they used to insert the memory implant is very much like a CAT scan machine and, once a sensitive, paranoid mind gets an idea, it is very easy for it to be realistically incorporated into that person's own thoughts. Any type of delusion can be lodged in a person's mind. You can think you are a secret agent, a hockey player, a great lover – you name it. Only time and the proper medication can make it all go away and there are many forms of this illness and probably just as many differing types of medications.

The right ones, with a good doctor, can work miracles. Medications that are slightly wrong for you can make you feel horrible, gain so much weight or sleep so much that you barely have anything close to a normal life. Unfortunately, I was a long way from understanding that, eventually, I would get well again and it was the medication that would do it.

The ward I was on was called 9B-South and it had the distinction of being the most violent, filthy and heart-breaking, will-snapping places in the entire hospital complex. The floors were constantly dusty; the windows were mostly painted shut and had greasy handprints on them. The few windows that were low enough looked out on grounds that were, at that time, as depressing as the smoke-stained, undecorated walls. They looked out on bare trees and a thick coating of snow, an impossible barrier to us because they wouldn't let us have our own coats. The whole ward was a cramped, long hallway painted in a dingy and cracking eggshell white, with dorm rooms for male and female, a television room that had walls so coated with nicotine stains it was hard to tell the original color of the paint. When you went to 9B South you stayed inside usually in increments of weeks or months, rarely getting a glimpse of the doctors, all the time sucking in that smoke and institutional air.

Everywhere you went, there was the army of the great unwashed, all wanting one thing and one thing only — cigarettes. I remember one person they brought in. A nice guy they had found him somewhere outside with no shoes on. When they brought him in, his swollen and frozen feet looked like they were going to fall off and he had a large brown paper bag full of $20 bills. He would often walk a couple of steps and then fall asleep while still standing.

Everyone in there was heartbreaking, from the old native guy who kept drawing crude pictures of military equipment and mailing them to the recruiting centre, to the young woman who came in because of her addictions, seven months pregnant.

9B-South included half of the top floor of a building made for returning First World War soldiers who had gone insane overseas. All the windows had a wire mesh over them, through which you could see the grounds but you couldn't go out and walk through them. All the doors had ancient, impenetrable locks that would stand up to any patient who tried to get through.

Violence came at you from different directions in that place. If you were rude or uncooperative to the staff, often your punishment would be getting wrestled to the ground (often slammed to the ground) and being injected with a substance that caused the seizure of all of your muscles and a general feeling of all-around nausea in the extreme. You could be then either set free or, if they felt like it, they would put you in what they called "the side room," which was a white room with a hard floor and a window high and out of reach. You would sit in there for hours until they felt like releasing you.

I thought such things were only in old prison novels or in stories of Korean War prison camps but here it was happening to me. I didn't have a clue that such a place could exist in Canada and it was a huge shock to now be in it. All that had to happen was for one staff member to decide you should be punished, in whatever way they chose that day, and it was done.

As an example, I went up to the nursing station and tried to wait patiently to get someone's attention. All the staff members were casually talking and laughing when one of them walked right up to me and tried to close the door in my face. I didn't think before speaking, I just said, "hey — fuck off!" and for using that word, I was slammed to the floor, injected, and thrown in the side room. As I was lying on the floor, I asked why they were doing this and the reply came, "because you don't talk that way to women!" Such punishments had an air of Nazism to them.

The other violence was violence from the patients. One time, I was in a dorm room and the person across the hallway from me was vomiting on the floor. I asked him to go to the bathroom to do that so he ran across and started punching me. Another time, I got into a fistfight with a rather large young man over a picture of an actress on the cover of a magazine. He said he could have her any time and I said he couldn't, and it came to blows. There was no peace to be had, in any part of this locked-down ward, and it was so scary being lumped in with these people not knowing if I would ever get out. Every request a person made to see their doctor would elicit the response of "tomorrow," but tomorrow never came unless you were doing really well.

My doctor tried to explain to me that I had an illness that made me go into highs and lows (bipolar or manic-depression is the definition, but for some reason in modern psychiatry doctors are reluctant to ever come out with a diagnosis, not so much for the benefit of the patient, more likely due to fear of misdiagnosis and a lawsuit) and that I needed medications to help smooth out the hills and valleys in my mood. I didn't see things that way at all, didn't believe him and tried to explain that I had a close friend kill himself and had a lot of family problems, especially with my dad.

These things were true but, sadly, they weren't the cause of my strange behaviours or my delusions that I was some kind of special being. I thought I was hiding those things well. An occasional aspect of my illness made it so I thought I had to hide those feelings. I thought if the doctors knew what was really going on in my head they would never let me out of that horrible place. So, I kept all my pain, all my delusions, all my fears deep down inside, only thinking of the day I would be on the other side of the bars.

Day after day went on and I kept everything bottled up. I used knowledge I had gleaned from stories I had read and seen about prisons and tried to just keep my mind on the six inches in front of my face and nothing else. One of the things I would do was brush my teeth, over and over, trying to focus on that task and not think about where I was or what was happening to me. Somehow I felt if I used this trick (one I learned at survival camp), I would get through. I forget how long it took but, as the medications they were giving me began to work a bit, and I had less

Through The Withering Storm

"incidents" with the staff, I was transferred off of 9B-South.

I was put into a less severe ward called 10-1A and the time seemed to go a little faster. I still thought I had some obligation to be a tough guy, though, and I would talk down to other people, make bets on pool games knowing I would win, and generally try to be as much of a pain in the ass as I could.

A young nurse on 10-1A seemed to be attracted to me. She didn't say much, but once she came into the washroom while I was having a shower, pulled open the curtain and stood talking to me and quite obviously staring at me for a couple of minutes while I was naked. Another time the same nurse came into the bathroom in my room and again caught me naked. When I think of that now, it was kind of a gross feeling to have her stare at me, something unwanted, though at the time it was an ego boost.

I spent my days working with wood in occupational therapy, again trying to keep that focus I used when I was on 9B-South. I also spent some time talking with psychologists and doing questionnaires for them. I even got some of my grade 10 math correspondence finished. In a relatively short time, I was told that, as long as I took my medications, I could go home and go back to school. I was greatly relieved to have appeared sane enough to be let out, especially since I was still harboring a great deal of anger at my admission to this dungeon in the first place. One Friday my dad came to drive me home to St. Albert, and that was that.

One of my major beefs about being incarcerated was that I had been taking a lot of abuse from my dad and it didn't seem fair that I was being labeled ill when it wasn't really my fault. No one took what I said to heart until just about my last day there, when my dad was on his way to pick me up. A nurse came up to me and told me that she had similar problems, saw a counselor about them and it really helped. She was a young and pretty nurse and really did her job well, so it really impressed me that she would go out of her way to help me like that. Up until then, it didn't seem like the staff was there to help me at all.

On our way home, we encountered a funeral procession and my spinning head decided that "they" had known I was on that route and had put on the procession for my dead friend, Glen. I started crying and for a few minutes my dad didn't really know what to do, he didn't even say anything, just let my delusions and illusions ride free. We got back to the house and the first thing I did was get a cold beer from the fridge. When the alcohol had set in a little, I called up Wendy, the girl from my French class. I told her I loved her and that I was falling apart and needed to meet her and talk but she flatly refused. She said she could be my friend but she was involved with someone else.

I called another friend and got him to come get me and take me to a bar way on the other side of Edmonton. I went to a couple of bars and then ended up at a place a lot of people from my old high school went. I was standing near the entrance and lo and behold here was Mandy, the hot babe from junior high I was once in love with, and man did she look good. I don't know why but she just ooohed and ahhhed over me and all at once I was in love again. I was too nervous to talk to her and I ended up walking away. Then, I got excessively drunk in another part of the bar and decided to go find her and ask her to dance. When I found her, she was kissing a guy from our high school who I really didn't like, so I ended up

Through The Withering Storm

feeling like an ass and getting myself even drunker. I got so inebriated I had to call information twice to get a number for a cab and then ended up taking another person's cab to get home. I spent a great deal of money that day but there was one solace. It was all money I had gotten from filing a grievance about my last employer. That little case was about the closest I was ever to get to being a lawyer and it paid off. Enough to get wasted at least.

The next few days were a whirlwind of events. After quitting cold turkey and going three months without a cigarette, I started smoking again for the simple reason that I felt I could keep in touch with members of the 'network,' the people who were part of the false alliances I had invented in my sick mind. I went back to school smoking up a storm and only lasted three days. On the third day I kept thinking that I had some destiny, some special mission to accomplish and then all of a sudden I was presented with an opportunity.

My gym class was playing hockey when I got back to school and one of the guys on the ice with me was Wendy's boyfriend, who had been nothing but a gentleman to me in all the time I knew him. Out of the blue, my thoughts told me that he was to be destroyed. I set in after him and beat him up pretty badly. While I was doing this, the whole class came up and pounded on the Plexiglas just like in a real hockey game and I pounded harder, putting on a real show. In that one moment, I had changed from a simple, book-loving student to a raging, ferocious animal hungry for blood. I could literally feel my heart pounding, my anger rising. I had not had any fights in school up to that point and now I was doing something I couldn't even imagine if I weren't so sick.

Some guys stopped the fight and asked me why I had done it. My answer didn't make sense to anyone. I think I said something like, "he's the guy who has been fucking with me!" or something to that effect. My gym teacher took me in his car and drove me back to the school. All he wanted to do was find Wendy so I could talk to her or perhaps so he and the guidance counselor and I could talk to her.

We waited at the office for the guidance counselor and I saw a poster about schizophrenia. I read it aloud for some reason, but nothing sank in. I had no idea what schizophrenia was even though I was likely at that moment suffering from every symptom of it. I was ill. I believed I hadn't just spent a month in a mental hospital because I had a problem. I was just someone under pressure who had never stood up for himself. The extent of how these "thoughts" could trick me was unbelievable.

After a few minutes, the counselor came and gave me a sheet with Wendy's class schedule and phone number and I didn't know what to do with it. I just sat there staring at him, not saying a word. A lot of people used to say that when they dealt with me when I was sick like that they didn't really know what was going on. They weren't alone. I didn't even know what was going on myself or what to do and I still had a small voice inside me telling me to do horrible things.

After a few seconds, the counselor went through his second door to the school office and I went with him. There they all were – the principal, the counselor, my grade coordinator and all the school administrators. When I refused to say anything, my grade coordinator, who used to buy his gas at the gas station I worked at all summer, said to me, "Leif, I thought we were friends."

Through The Withering Storm

"You aren't my friend. I've never seen you before in my life," I replied, in all sincerity. I think the main reason I said this was because the guy who asked the question used to be a cop and I had instantly thought he was going to play a mind game with me.

"Call the police," he said and the guidance counselor ran off like a scared rabbit.

A few minutes passed and then two RCMP officers came to the room. I stood up straight like a soldier and quietly went with them. I had figured that how I was going to take it, no point in trying to resist the law. But then, as we rounded the corner exiting the office, there was the entire school lined up in the hallway. It was not unlike a "march of shame" and I decided I wasn't going to take it lying down. Taking a lesson from my brother, I grabbed one of the officers and used him like a pendulum to smash into the other. Then, I slammed the second cop into the wall. All the way down the hall, we fought and wrestled in front of the silent crowd that had gathered.

Not all of them really mattered to me, but I remember as they were dragging me out after putting an extremely painful hold onto my neck, I saw a girl named Lisa. She was a beautiful young brunette who had also been in that same French class with Wendy. Years later while I was dealing with problems inside my own head I heard that she had been engaged (way after graduation) to that same guy I had beat up and she had been an anorexic which caused her to die of a heart attack. I don't understand how cruel this world can be. My prayers go out to that guy. He had never done anything wrong to me, it was all my sick mind's own creation that made me want to hurt him.

The police took me to the local hospital again; I was again injected forcibly and taken in the back of a patrol car to the institution. If I had gone quietly, I would have been taken to the ward for less serious cases. They actually tried to take me there but, when I got there, they threw me into a phone booth. I didn't really know what to do but I had a scrap of paper with Wendy's phone number on it so I tried to call it but her brother answered and told me never to call again. I forget what happened from there but there was some screaming and more manhandling of yours truly and I was brought back to 9B-South.

I ended up spending a long time in that ward because I really was a mess. I was battered and bruised and now a heavy smoker and even less compliant than before. I didn't think he cared much at all, but was told by my brother-in-law that my dad was very traumatized by all that was happening to me. Amazingly, no matter how much we argued, or how much we got angry at each other, my dad felt that it was just a teenage phase I was going through. I found out later that every day I was in the hospital, he had an extremely hard time talking about me and was often found crying his eyes out. He visited every day and was a tower of strength when it came to dealing with all the stuff he had on his plate. At the same time all of this had happened, my mom was attending university and ended up getting very sick. I can only imagine the turmoil my dad was going through at the time.

The worst thing about 9B-South wasn't the patients, the abusive staff or the psychiatrists who would often leave you there for weeks or more before they would see you to even discuss being transferred. The worst thing about it was there was so little to do. There was no pool table because people soon discovered pool cues and pool balls are good weapons. We couldn't have a lot of personal items and often weren't even allowed a belt or shoelaces.

Through The Withering Storm

You also had to light your cigarettes at the office and then take them into the smoking room.

So, if you wanted something to do, you smoked but so many of the people there were locked away from any means of getting money for cigarettes. I had family and a bit of money left from my job, so I still had a fairly steady supply of smokes. This was not always a good thing because with so little to do you could run through a carton in two to three days.

During that time, my dad sold my precious .22 caliber rifle. I spent so much time using it that it had become like an old familiar pipe or a walking stick to me. Now, of course, I understand that someone in my state shouldn't have a gun but my rifle had meant a lot to me in the days when I was young and alone, when I would go out to some unpopulated area and hunt rabbits.

The sale of my rifle mostly supplied my smoking habit for a little while but I was one of the lucky ones. If you had cigarettes, you had to guard them with your life. I can remember a guy coming up to me every half hour asking if I would lend him one. Finally, as I sat puffing on a cigarette I told him I didn't smoke and he went away. An hour later, he came back. I got so sick of it I would start asking for stuff in return for smokes and, before long, I had a real collection of junk — Gideon bibles, cheap rings and so on.

There were a lot of characters in 9B-South. One was a lady who had the appearance of a down-on-her-luck streetwalker. One day, she came into the smoking room and said to me, "Vern, I know who you are now. I remember you from that dance so you better not play any more of your tricks." It seems funny now but at the time I was scared. It's odd to think of people in high school who don't want to be friends with someone because they have out-of-style clothes or because they are overweight or a number of silly reasons. Here I was lumped in with people who had done heaven knows what.

I was to find out later that just about all of the murderers and child molesters were in a part of the hospital specially made to be a prison for the criminally insane and where I was, with the staff to patient ratio and other factors, made it fairly safe. It was so hard at the time for me to accept the fact that I was not as different from these people as I thought. Many of them had good families and somewhat normal lives before ending up in that hospital. Very few of them had any intention of hurting me or anyone. We all suffered together and there was a lot more of "those people" than I had ever imagined.

I will never forget a time long after these events when I was visiting a friend who worked at a gas station and a couple of girls came in. I was talking with my friend and as they came in I started talking to them, made a joke and they just looked at me like I was a piece of garbage who shouldn't dare talk to such royalty. One of them said, well within my hearing range, "we're not in St. Albert anymore." That was a real shocker to me, that in just a couple of short years I had become the unwanted. And it didn't help to remind me that I had been, in a way, "cast out" of the hometown I so dearly loved.

I often wonder how I made people feel when I was younger and I had been rude to someone and really hurt them through some kind of elitist attitude, like these girls had done to me. After so many years of being sick, I didn't begin to get better until I accepted that I was no better than anyone else, especially my fellow sufferers. That was when the tables really turned for me.

Through The Withering Storm

Time passed. Up and down the institution hallways, I walked. Back and forth, back and forth, counting the tiles, looking into the designs for secret messages. Sitting in the smoking room thinking the sound of the air conditioner was a military tattoo calling me to go out in the hall and claim the Congressional Medal of Honor. I spent as much time as I could watching television, sleeping, and eating French fries. Anything else could cause me to let go, to give in to the constant voices and invasive thoughts.

I clung to little things, little routines and habits, like trying to always get the same color tray at meal times. Somehow this was comfort to me, watching the colors go by, walking closer and closer to the end of the food line where some crap would slap onto my plate with a loud "glop."

The delusions dogged me and a fight started because I heard voices in my head. Then things started to stabilize. Two weeks went by and the voices were quiet, three weeks and the things I did at school no longer seemed rational to me, though they had seemed the only logical course of action at the time. Then a month passed and I was let out of the hospital again like a prisoner on probation.

Once again, I was given strict instructions to take my medication as prescribed, and see my doctor on a regular basis. Once again, I failed to heed this advice and went off to do my own thing, still living with my parents, eating their food and taking up their space, time and energy, getting into constant disagreements with my dad.

One of the first significant things I did was get myself a job at the plastics plant where I had earned the money to buy my Cobra a year before. There was to be no more school for me. I had been told by my principal that he couldn't allow me to come back because I had missed too much of that school year but I could come back the next year. I responded by calling him up out of the blue and telling him to fuck off for no apparent reason. The plastics plant phoned me back and I started work within a couple of days.

    When I had worked for them previously, I fit in well and did good work. After a few hundred buckets come out of a machine, you develop a rhythm to doing things. This time, though, I must have been greatly affected by my medications because no such rhythm developed. I had a bad case of the shakes in my hands and I didn't have nearly the motor control that I did earlier. The medications had saved my life but at great expense. After three days, I was fired for not working fast enough so I went back to the old routine of staying up all night watching TV and scrounging everything I could just to keep myself smoking. My one comfort was that my three days of work would give me enough to buy smokes for a few more days. After that, I had no idea what I would do. Options were limited in the town I lived in.

    My dad was not terribly pleased at my lifestyle and what it was costing to run the lights and the TV all night, not to mention the microwaved hot dogs I was consuming. The only real light in the tunnel, at that point, was that I still had a few friends who were willing to talk with me and hang out with me. I was also lucky because my sister's boyfriend did me a great favor by selling me back my old motorbike for $1 so I could at least get around.

    My old friend Lurch was one of the few who stuck by my side, and he also drove a motorbike. Lurch was a 6' 4", wore black leather with studs and chains and scared everyone he came near. I liked the idea of that because I feared reprisals from the people

Through The Withering Storm

I had gone to school with. I had already heard a report from a policeman friend of mine that I had been accused of attempting to rape a woman, which was completely fabricated. I also feared the friends of the guy I had beat up and others like him.

Lurch and I did a lot of cruising that summer. We would go anywhere in any weather. I felt like an outcast when I was around people my own age but, when he and I rode together, we were two free spirits with no limits to what we could do.

A short while later I got a job at a gas station just inside the city of Edmonton. I was going to be trained to work the night shift which I thought would be fun, hoping that I would have a lot of time to read. I was in a terrible mental state, though, when I worked there. I was angry at the world, at all the people who never seemed to give a rip about me. My moral compass was broken and my formerly fine-tuned manners had disappeared.

We had a big sign up by the propane pumps saying Cylinder refill $2. If someone came in and asked for a refill, I would give them one for the stated price. But, if someone came in and asked how much a refill was I figured they hadn't seen the sign, so I would charge them $5 and pocket the difference. I didn't work there for very long either.

While I was there, a guy on my block invited me over to meet two girls he had visiting. They were pretty but kind of young. They claimed they were both 15 but I didn't take that at face value. We watched a movie together and somehow we got them to agree to play strip poker. The girl who was supposed to be with me lost big time and was naked in a few hands. When she got up to go upstairs I remember her having a sexy butt that had a white triangle on it — tan lines from a bikini. The guy, whose parents' house it was, went up after her and was gone for a while.

Meanwhile, I went on playing with the girl downstairs and got her naked as well. Normally, this would have been a dream come true but somehow I didn't want to lose my virginity to a girl of questionable morals who was possibly underage. Also, I don't think there were any condoms around and with an HIV scare circulating the world plus all the other possibilities, I wisely refrained from going too far. I settled for necking and left things at that.

A couple of days after that my dad and I got into a real serious fight and he called the police, so I took off to Edmonton in hopes of staying with an old friend. Somehow, I found his apartment and the next day I went around looking for jobs nearby. After a long day, we sat down for a beer. My friend called up his girlfriend and introduced us over the phone. Turned out she had gone to school with me and I was telling her all about being in the hospital and having problems at home. She sounded like she really wanted to help me, even offered a place to stay but I was totally headstrong and honestly thought I could stay with my buddy.

Not much later that night he told me he didn't think things would work out in the whole roommate situation because he smoked drugs and I smoked cigarettes. I practically had to beg him to give me a ride to my army friend's house, which he eventually did. Later that night, I decided the one thing I could do to really turn my life around would be to join the army with him.

My army friend helped me force down a few of our favorite cocktails, which were Caesars (made the Canadian way with Clamato juice and vodka, salt in the drink and on the rim of the glass). We got nicely toasted and I got him to shave my head. What did it matter anymore, I thought, as he took off my last symbols of normalcy. Everyone I knew had cast me out, made me out to be some kind of monster. I might as well look the part. The next day I was down at the recruiting centre, ready to volunteer while a war was brewing in the Persian Gulf. They weren't open that day and my army friend wanted to go back to his barracks in Calgary and so, with the last of my cash, I bought a return ticket to Calgary and off we went.

Life on the base was interesting to say the least. I felt like I was committing some kind of crime being there. When we got to his room, there was a beer fridge and two cold ones waiting for us. For a couple of days, we went around Calgary seeing the sights and trying in vain to pick up women. One strong memory from this time is that my army friend had a close buddy who had tried to quit drinking and, while I was there, gave in, and knocked back 11 beers in one sitting. A short time later he got into a drunk driving accident and lost his left leg. There, but for the grace of God, go I.

When my friend's leave ended, I had to make my way back to Edmonton somehow and couldn't for the life of me find my bus ticket. I had never done it before but I decided the only thing for me to do would be to hitch-hike. My brother had told me stories about hitchhiking and said a person should try things from that angle at least once. I took the city bus as far north as it would get me and then set off. I walked a long way, likely about six to eight kilometers before anyone stopped to pick me up. Maybe the shaved head scared them off but eventually a guy stopped and he also picked up another hitchhiker who was just a bit further down the road. It was lucky, too, because it was starting to rain and I had no raincoat or anything with me.

LEIF GREGERSEN

    I feel really bad now but at the time I looked down on the other guy my ride picked up. He was obviously mentally ill and was just a very simple person. He mentioned that he had a paper route that paid for his living and I made rude comments back to him. When we were let off I asked him if he had ever been in hospital and he said no, but then I asked him if he had been in Ponoka and he said yes. My mom was there when she was a young woman and she told me horror stories about things such as shock treatments administered without anesthetic, causing people to scream blue bloody murder. I should have felt sorry for this guy but I was just a young dumb 18-year-old.

    That first ride only got me halfway to Edmonton but the second got me close to home. It was a big 18-passenger van that picked me up and I was dying for a smoke not having had one in hours. I managed to reach behind me to the ashtray on the back of the seat I was sitting in and pick out a few choice butts to roll up the tobacco left in them. When we got to Edmonton, I gave the guy wrong directions so I could be let off closer to where my brother worked. I got in touch with my brother and he agreed to let me stay for a night. I was just about ready to collapse once I got there carrying a big duffle bag I had half-filled with books, not knowing where I was going or where I would end up.

    It seemed like everything I did in those days was a scam, trying to take things that weren't mine or manipulate people and situations to my advantage. I think that had a lot to do with me just not caring after being in the hospital but also having no role models other than what I had seen in movies, in which the ability to run scams, cheat, lie and steal were all glorified. My dad was an extremely honest, hardworking and dedicated person but my brother-in-law had poisoned me against him, with all his left-wing rhetoric.

At my brother's place, I had a bit of trouble sleeping so I picked up a book he had lying around that I had heard about. It was Robert M. Pirsig's *Zen and the Art of Motorcycle Maintenance*. I just couldn't stop reading it. I think I went through 200 of its 380 pages before I got too tired to go on. It was such an eye opener for me, the very first time I had ever heard of a story about someone who had suffered from a mental illness and was still able to accomplish something so great as to write a book that changed a generation. I vowed to finish the book as soon as I found another copy. The journey to find one was to prove to be extremely long and hard.

The next day I took the bus back to St. Albert and hoped my dad had cooled off a bit. Unfortunately he hadn't. I managed to placate my parents a bit by convincing them that I was joining the army and that it would be good for me, which bought me a little time. Not long after coming back, though, my dad got blisteringly mad at me and kicked me out again. I knew he was serious but I didn't know what to do. I was quickly running out of friends I could stay with and hated the idea of being a sponge to anyone and their family. My dad's house was the only place I had ever lived.

I went to corner store and tried to think up some kind of a plan. What happened next was one of the most horrible things anyone has ever done to me. Right there at the store, in front of my friends, an RCMP officer arrested me. He took me to the police station where my parents were waiting in another room and told me my dad was charging me with trespassing.

I was devastated and heartbroken but I wasn't stupid. He had done a few things to me in my day and I was ready to use them if he wanted to carry through with the charge. I told the officer that if he was going to charge me with trespassing, he had better also charge my dad with assault. He left for a while. When he came back, he told me I was free to go.

I made my way back to my neighborhood and ended up going over to the house of the guy who threw the strip poker party. He said very little, let me in his car, along with a girl or two he had with him and then drove about 30 km to the south side of Edmonton. When we got there, he turned to me and said, "get out."

"What do you mean get out?"

"I mean leave."

"You asshole. You can't just drive someone to the middle of nowhere and kick them out. All the fucking favors I have done you, all the places I drove you and you do this!" I could have killed him.

I managed to get bus fare from one of the girls and rode the bus downtown. I was told about a hostel where a person could stay for free but ended up at a youth hostel instead. The desk clerk gave me directions to the free hostel where I was supposed to be. This place was the filthiest dungeon I had ever seen. I was put in a room with a dozen other guys who were snoring away and stinking up the place. Nowhere was a person safe with any tobacco. The next day I went out and rented the first room I could find that welfare would pay for. I hated the idea of being on welfare but justified it by telling myself I was leaving for the army soon. I ended up with a 10 x 10' room that had no soundproofing, a bathroom down the hall, cracking and peeling paint everywhere and a mattress that seemed like it had been used as a diaper. Home.

Despite living in squalor, I did push myself to train for the army. I was running all the time. I eventually bought a bike and took out a membership in a gym. I went to a placement agency and got temporary work with a plumbing supply company. The thing that really got to me was the feeling of being downtown among all the high towers and busy streets, while somewhere off in the distance (literally and figuratively) another school year was starting without me. As an academic who had hoped to be in university at this time, the feeling nearly broke my heart. I found solace in reading all the books I could in my free time. One book that really hit me was *On the Road* by Jack Keroac.

Aside from working and reading, I had a lot of duties to fulfill in order to be accepted by the military. To discover if I had what it took to learn a second language, I was tested in Amish after being taught a few key phrases. I passed test after test and then, as they were starting to talk about where we wanted to be posted and what kind of goals we had, I was asked about 150 questions by an army doctor. After about 100 of them he asked me a simple yes or no question. If I had lied and said no, I would have gone in but I said yes. The question was, "Have you ever seen a psychiatrist or a psychologist?"

With my honest answer, they put everything on hold and waited for me to get a full report from my doctor. I was working out of town for an oil company when I got the word. I had been treated with lithium and, once you have been on lithium, you can never join the military. It didn't matter that when I was in the hospital there was a paratrooper who had punched out a major and had been on lithium when they sent him back. It didn't matter that I had passed all the tests and that my doctor felt joining the military would be good for me. I was a psycho and they didn't need me.

At that point I felt a little numb, a little sad and a little happy. I was numb because I wasn't even good enough to get a shot at a military career. I was sad because I wasn't going to have a big adventure to tell my grandkids about and I was happy because I didn't have to go to war and die.

My next plan was to leave. Leave everything, all the pain and the memories and a father I couldn't get along with, a mother I dearly loved and friends who never seemed to give a shit. I was headed west on a thumb and a prayer – headed for Vancouver, and the Promised Land.

I didn't have any specific plans on when I wanted to leave but the situation in my parent's home was so tense I kept a bag close by with sandwiches, water and a raincoat. I didn't have a clue about hitchhiking and I had never taken on such a journey. I knew little of where I was going except that it was by the sea and it wasn't Edmonton.

I stayed up in my room for most of one day. When my dad came home, he was furious that I hadn't done anything and that, since I slept all day again, I would again be awake all night, using his electricity and eating hot dogs. That was how my decision to leave was made. Over 30 cents worth of hot dogs and 10 cents worth of electricity. We had a severe argument. My dad threatened to have me put back in the hospital and I threatened to punch him in the face if he didn't give me a fair chance to get away. I walked out and wasn't arrested. Not long after, I set out down the road, was picked up and given a ride to the main highway that would eventually lead to Vancouver.

I had a long way to go. Vancouver is about 1,200 km from Edmonton so I had to rely on a succession of rides to take me there. My resolve was to make it to the coast or die trying. Nothing was going to stop me. It took me four or five rides but, by morning, I had made it to the small tourist town of Jasper which was about 400 km. west of Edmonton. I was cold, tired and nearly gave in.

Walking along a highway was scary. Of course I was alone, which didn't scare me much because I was used to that, but the idea that some vicious animal could pop up and maul me at any time didn't make me feel too comfortable. However, the concept of going back and into the mental hospital again was an overpowering reason to keep going no matter what obstacles lay ahead.

When I got to Jasper, I phoned the youth hostel and nearly booked a room with the intentions of resting up and turning around to go back to my parent's house. But the pain my dad caused me was extremely fresh in my memory. I did need some rest so, for as long as I could, I went into the train station and slept in a chair, trying not to look like the transient I was. After a couple of hours of rest, I sucked up my courage and headed out further on the highway. I had also thought of buying a ticket to Vancouver with my last $70 but I decided against it.

Not far outside of Jasper, a very kind man from Calgary picked me up. We talked for a long time, as the incredible mountain scenery rolled past us. He was a Christian and a member of the Gideon society. Even though I wasn't a Christian at that point in my life, I found him very easy to talk to. When he let me off he gave me a small bible and his phone number and told me I could call him any time I needed something. At the time, I was still an atheist but open to new ideas and, whatever this gentleman had, I wanted some of it. He had some kind of inner peace and happiness that I had sought after but never held onto for any length of time. I had seen it before but never felt very worthy of it. Now that I was far from the anger and the demands of home, I had a change of heart and resolved to learn more about Jesus and the book I had been given.

    In the town where my ride dropped me off, I stopped and had a meal, bought some cigarettes and walked off down the highway, now even more determined that I was going to make it to the coast. As I left the town, I witnessed a sight that left me breathless for just a moment, just long enough to make the whole journey worthwhile. The sky was half clear and half full of cumulonimbus clouds framing the snow capped Rocky Mountains, which stood above a dried lakebed in which two moose were running. The beautiful scene seemed to encapsulate the whole concept of something that lived its whole life in the wild. I stood and took it all in, with part of me wishing I had been born an animal that never had to get wrestled down and locked up, that could run free in such a place of beauty. This whole trip had been teaching me things that before I would have said were impossible earlier in the year. From the two moose, I learned that the appreciation of nature and beauty was still there, had never left, but had, perhaps, become faint for a while.

    Not long after that, I caught another ride, this time with an older gentleman from Kamloops. He was a real talker. It was easy to see why he picked me up. This was a long lonely ride for him and he loved to tell stories. He talked about when he moved to

Through The Withering Storm

B.C., his business, his family. I would have really enjoyed all this but we were cruising through mountain roads often with no guard rails and thousands of feet of air in between the road and the bottom of the valleys. On top of that, he had a water jug beside him that he filled mostly with water but partially with whiskey. Still, he proved to be a capable driver and when we finally got to Kamloops near nightfall, he went way out of his way to let me off closer to town.

In Kamloops, I stopped at a buffet and spent a few more of my precious dollars on a bit of food. I filled up as much as I could and hiked up a huge mountain road trying to get a ride. It didn't help much that all over the place there were signs saying "No hitch-hiking, fine for pickup." The warning didn't stop me from trying, until I saw a patrol car coming, dove into some brush and hid myself. I walked on, up the massive mountain road and across the highway. After a while, the walking started to get to me. My knees were in pain and my feet were worse, after 10 or 11 hours of this constant walking. I was actually hoping to be arrested and sent to a nice warm jail cell. No such luck.

I walked until finally I couldn't walk any more. I hiked off into some trees by the side of the road and used my cadet survival skills to first build a fire and then try to get some sleep. I did sleep a bit, but it was totally restless sleep. I remember at one point I woke up and was half aware that I was in the mountains while the other half mistakenly thought I was safely camping out in the back yard of my parents' home. The waking up and realizing part of that dream was awful.

In the morning, I set out determined to get myself a ride or walk to the next town. By a stroke of luck, I was picked up within about 10 minutes of getting back on the road. This ride was with a 25-year-old man driving a convertible MGB and we got along really well. He didn't have tire chains and so we had to take an alternate route to Vancouver because parts of the highway we were on were snowed in. Just for fun we put on our toques, let the top down and had the most amazing view of the mountains as we careened down the old Trans-Canada highway.

    I had been down this road a few times as a kid but it was never this much fun. My driver had lived in Hope, B.C. where they had shot the film Rambo with Sylvester Stallone, so we stopped in there for a while to look for bullet holes and then went climbing through a bunch of caves that had once been a tourist attraction. They were known as the Sasquatch Caves and I had been in them when I was a young boy 15 years ago.

    A couple of more hours on the highway went by and I was flabbergasted to find that it was green and raining in Vancouver. I had expected it would be snowy and drab like Edmonton at that time of year but, back then, I obviously didn't understand much about coastal cities. My ride was nice enough to take me right to the door of a very inexpensive travelers' hostel and I booked a bed for the night. They didn't have much room so I ended up sleeping on a couch in a living room that I shared with two Danish women who had just graduated from nursing school. I felt bad about it but it had taken me more than two days to get there and I only brought one pair of thick wool socks that were soaked with stinking sweat. Overnight, they dried up and left a terrible thick stench in the room so bad a person could barely breathe. But I had made it to Vancouver.

Through The Withering Storm

I had no money, no friends in town, didn't know my way around, but I had made it. I thought that meant I could leave everything behind me but, sadly, most of the bad stuff had come right along with me. The memories, all the pain and the loneliness were right there between my ears the whole time. There was no running from an illness like mine or the hurt that had brought me across the Rocky Mountains.

At that point, I felt my life didn't count for much.

Chapter Seven: Riding a Roller Coaster

My first few days in Vancouver were a real culture shock. Just walking down the dirty and dingy street the hostel was on, I could still see the harbor and the mountains of the North Shore. It was such a pretty city though I viewed the 'pretty' parts of it from what is actually the poorest neighborhood in Canada, an area called the downtown East Side. Even with that, it was so much more alive than Edmonton ever was. I did feel kind of bad, though, because when I finally phoned home my mom was worried sick about me. I was very close to my mom and I had felt that leaving Edmonton meant figuratively leaving her to die. But in reality, she and my dad, now without any kids around, had a chance to renew their relationship and were doing better than ever.

A few days went by and I made friends with a couple of people. With their help and by asking around, I found out about a government labor placement agency not far from the hostel. One morning, I woke up early and struck out for this place.

Vancouver's downtown East Side had many similarities to the typical hallways in a mental hospital. This whole part of town had the aura of mental illness about it. The people were the forgotten, the homeless, the downtrodden and poor. It is a sad indictment of our system to know that this is what we do to people who have a medical problem, one that affects the brain. The words of one man who spoke to me around this time while reading the newspaper will always stay with me. He said "All I read are the hockey scores and the UFO stories. Everything else is bullshit."

Through The Withering Storm

By some stroke of luck or maybe because I was one of the few desperate for any job, I got sent out my very first day to a job on a construction site. At the end of the day, I was paid $56 for my efforts and was asked to come back the next day. I liked the guys I was working with and the job wasn't anything too difficult, so I agreed. I was in good shape to handle the work because I had been running upwards of 30 kilometers a week at that point, along with full workouts. When I got back to the hostel, though, the owner had put up a sign on my door that read: "Leif — pay now or move out!" I paid up and felt a great sense of accomplishment that I had done all this on my own.

My only real escape from the hostile world of Main Street and Terminal Avenue was my running. Somewhere in the back of my mind I knew, because of my mental illness, that I couldn't get into the military but still I wanted to train. Maybe I could become an athlete, even an amateur one. By that time, I loved sports, though my chances to play them were getting fewer and farther between. Even though I smoked, I tried to run every kilometer I could handle, heading out for 10 km runs just to punish myself.

I saw those runs as my penance, my pain-payment for all the lousy things I had done to people back home. I was starting to tentatively believe in a higher power and from what I had seen in movies, this was how you achieved forgiveness. A part of me did want to get into the army and be sent to the Persian Gulf. It had seemed so much nobler to die a hero than a crazy suicidal maniac that a lot of people back home, even former close friends, thought I was now. Not a lot of what I was doing made sense but I kept going.

Most of my free time in that hostel was spent talking to and listening to a bunch of people who were traveling the four corners of the world. When it got dark I would go out and do my runs. Then, when I got back, I would hear some amazing tales. It seemed so exciting that these people could risk everything, travel everywhere and see all the things they had seen. Aside from a trip to my dad's country of Denmark and another to Disneyland, both around the age of 10, I really hadn't been anywhere.

After working a couple of weeks, I found a notice saying that a fellow was going to Seattle and would take passengers for a share of the cost of gas. This sounded great so I called him and booked a ride. The trip was a lot of fun. One of the first things we did was visit the duty-free store on the U.S.-Canada border. All my life, I had seen cigarettes carefully stacked in displays where people couldn't reach them and they were always $30-$40 a carton. Here, at the duty-free, there were stacks and stacks of cartons right in the middle of the floor and they were $8 each. That kind of blew me away but so would a lot of things I saw and did on that trip.

My ride took me to the hostel in Seattle and I ended up sharing floor space with a bunch of other people as the hostel was filled to capacity that night. It was a nice, clean place, though, and I discovered then that Americans are some of the greatest people in the world, despite the fact that their government may not be all that kind. I met a man who had been a soldier during the Second World War and had started out the war in Pearl Harbor as a private. The war ended for him when he was wounded as a colonel at Normandy. He was a sweet old man but, sadly, he was reduced to trying to sell people books with his picture in it or anything he could sell such as cowboy shirts which he got from who knows where.

Saturday night, I was standing out in front of the hostel smoking when a brand new Ford Thunderbird pulled up. A man got out and asked me if I knew where the hostel was. The mentally ill part of me wanted to give him a long list of complicated directions but the cadet in me told him he had found it. He got out, bummed a smoke and we sat and talked for a long time. Jason was a really neat person, a Canadian from Montreal, a skier and hockey fan. I didn't think much of the whole exchange but was destined to run into him again.

Seattle was such a clean and vibrant city. It rained a lot there, like Vancouver, but it had a distinct flavor of being American despite being only two hours from Canada. One of the mornings I was there, I remember walking out on a long pier, getting a coffee and just soaking up the whole sea atmosphere as I sipped away. I also went to the famous Space Needle, which was a ton of fun. We have a tower like it in Calgary but the big difference is that the Seattle tower lets you go out in the open air, while the Calgary one is enclosed. I also remember going down to a place called Pike's Market and making up my lunch as I went along, buying a drink at one stand, a piece of fried chicken at another. Then I stopped to buy a banana and a sign said: "Bananas— 25 cents," so I handed the guy a quarter and he gave me back change. I told him, "No, they are a quarter, aren't they?"

"Don't worry man, I'm on your side!" came the reply. I don't really know what side he or I was on but if that side made things cheaper I wasn't going to argue.

Sunday evening my ride showed up as promised, only this time, instead of having two Frenchmen in the back, there was a young woman who was studying literature at the University of British Columbia. We talked extensively about books and poems nearly the whole way back, as the fantastic northern Washington scenery went by but I didn't get her number. A few weeks later, someone told me she had stopped in to see me but didn't leave a message or even a name. This was to later become fuel for my delusions because, when the desk clerk described her, I thought she was one of the wealthy young women who had once pursued me in St. Albert, and I conjured up all kinds of strange ideas from this one event.

Not long after that, Christmas season was upon us and, as many mentally ill people do at that time of year, I started to slide down a slippery slope. It began with old delusions running through my head, feelings that a politician or movie star was plotting against me, or that I had a vast fortune stashed somewhere and all I had to do was take a cab to the airport. It was really scary, especially when my mind was so far gone that I start to believe it. I started to do very strange things.

When I was still in the early stages of these problems, I ran into Jason from the Seattle hostel again, the one from Montreal. He trying to take me under his wing and had the impression that he could somehow help me 'get over' my illness. This was an incredibly kind and unselfish approach but it would prove impossible. I needed a psychiatrist as much as I needed a friend at that time. We did get to be really close friends, however. In that same hostel in Vancouver, we met two Australian girls, Sharon and Cassie, which we took to restaurants, hockey games and all over the place. On one occasion, Jason,

Through The Withering Storm

Sharon and I were walking in downtown Vancouver and out of nowhere a man came and asked us if we wanted our picture taken. We agreed and for some reason, above our heads, written in graffiti, was the word "Angels." It was kind of neat to think about the divine when I was that age but I really didn't know where I stood in the whole religious spectrum. I figured there was a devil, I figured there was a God and there were spirits (my mental illness showed me that). But I didn't really want to do anything about either possibility. It was so much easier to think of just being spiritual and leaving things at that.

    Eventually, Sharon and Cassie left to take their train to Banff. Jason and I didn't really want to let them go. We ended up dancing them out of sight and when they were gone we were quite sad, Jason a little more so because I think he was in love with Sharon.

    It was near that time that my condition began to deteriorate rapidly. I would sit for hours in a deep state of worry, feeling so desperately alone, smoking cigarette after cigarette. I told a guy at the hostel that I had problems and that I was supposed to be taking medications. He called the hospital and set up an appointment for me with a doctor, even gave me directions. When I got out the front door, though, I got the directions mixed up and ended up going to a bar, having a beer and walked out without paying for it. Then, when the next welfare cheques came out, I decided I was going to go home.

    I got on a bus and headed for the deep freeze. At first, I thought I was going to stay with family but the only person who would take me in was my brother, who only let me stay one day. My thoughts were all over the place. It was a personal hell because I didn't know what to say to anyone and I don't remember if I even had enough money, it had been so costly to get home. So, I went to the local traveler's hostel and booked in, hoping and praying that something would come up to save me. I was rapidly losing my mind and really should have been sent to a hospital. I started to believe that God had given me special powers to read people's minds and that again, like in school, if I followed a certain set of rules, I could never be stopped.

A couple of times, I called up my parent's house and spoke to them but, after what had happened the last Christmas, I was adamant about not going there. After a few days, I decided that I should go back to Vancouver, a costly mistake.

A few nights after I got back to the coast and the hostel, I went into a friend's room, started smoking his pot (which I very rarely touched) and had a thought force its way into my head that I had to assume my friend's identity and steal his briefcase. The hostel clerk stopped me, so I walked out in the street, dropped my wallet on the ground and sat down in a pile of garbage not knowing what to do next. The next thing I remember was waking up with my wallet in my bed at the hostel. I am fairly sure that, after what I had done, my friends from the hostel had followed me and somehow got me to come back.

Again, I made the decision that I had to go home and get some help. It was such delusional thinking. First, I thought going to Alberta would help and I got mad at my parents, then I thought going back to B.C. was the solution. Now, when I literally had nothing, I felt my best bet would be to cross the Rocky Mountains heading east again in the middle of winter. I got on the Skytrain, rode it to the last station, then hopped a fence. I went into a truck stop hoping either to catch a ride but I was exhausted. The

Through The Withering Storm

first thing I did was sit down, open up the bible I had from when I came from Edmonton, leaned my head back and closed my eyes. I must have looked quite vulnerable at that point because someone came up to me and put $20 in my hand and told me to go back where I came from. I ended up buying a ticket to Hope, where I figured I would have an easier time of getting a ride further on up the highway.

Hope was covered in snow when I got there and it was perhaps the most pristine, beautiful time to be in that part of the country. Everything seemed so clean and unspoiled. I walked through town and got a ride not far down the road. Mind you, it was a ride in the back of a pick-up but a ride nonetheless. This ride let me off in a small town and I went and had something to eat, managing to catch another ride without even leaving the property. This ride was from a native man and I don't know if he intentionally screwed me around, but getting back to the main highway after he let me off proved to be a real chore. I ended up in another small town only nothing was near me, nothing was open. I nearly froze to death before some truckers agreed to give me another ride. They let me off at a Greyhound station and I was going to call a friend in St. Albert and get him to wire me a ticket, but while I was trying to do this I noticed a man looking at me and making abusive and disparaging comments. I started to get really pissed off so, just to see if he really was looking at me, I gave him the finger. He jumped up and exploded with rage, saying I wasn't getting on the bus and he knew the bus driver and all sorts of shit. I walked out of the depot and down the road, figuring to just hitch a ride, and was quickly picked up. Only this time by the police.

The officer looked through my bags and took me to a social worker, who talked to my parents and arranged to pay for a bus ticket home. Really this was all good. The only thing that bugged me was that I was taken to the bus depot far off in Kamloops in the back of a police car like a common criminal. The ride was long and my brain was spinning in a million directions, but I got through and my dad even came to pick me up and take me home. I didn't know what would happen to me next but, at least, I was back in a place where some things made sense again.

Despite the tension, my dad agreed to let me stay at home and I agreed to move to a group home as soon as I could find one. I didn't want to go but didn't see any other option. I was seriously ill and kept having delusions, especially about having an immense fortune hidden somewhere. Friends would give me a ride home and I would sit in the back of their car thinking I was being taken to my mansion. Then, I would start to say all kinds of weird stuff when they took me to my parents' house.

One day, an old friend from cadets called and asked if I wanted a bit of work bouncing at a dance in a nearby town. I agreed to it and while I was working there, a couple of girls tried really hard to get my attention and dance with me. I attempted to say no but my friend said I could, so I went out on the dance floor with them, kissed them, grabbed their butts and somehow got away with it. It was a real surprise to me that these girls found me attractive. I had cheap clothes on, an ill-fitting baseball cap, and if they had talked to me for more than 60 seconds they would have discovered I was more than a little crazy. I was a long ways from the sports-car-driving, well-groomed 17-year-old of just two years ago. In the end, my friend told me that he couldn't hire me again because I started more fights than I broke up.

I didn't have much to do so I took the bus out to the big mall and walked around for a while. When I was waiting for the bus to take me back to St. Albert, I started talking with some pretty cute girls who were skipping school and were from St. Albert as well. A couple of days later, I ran into them again, we talked for a while and two of them gave me their phone numbers. We decided to get together but, when they came over, I had an auditory hallucination that they wanted to meet a friend of mine who hung out at the corner store a lot. I called him up and gave him their numbers over the phone and he ended up more confused than I was.

Not long after that, social services sent me a couple of cheques, one for rent and one for spending money. I kept the rent money and the spending money to myself and, for a separate reason, ended up fighting with my dad and getting kicked out again. I got a room at a local hotel and did all kinds of weird things. I kept trying doors on cars thinking they were mine. At one point, I took a cab to the home of a young woman I went to school with. All I accomplished was really annoying her dad. I had never met him but when he heard my name he practically exploded with rage. I really wanted to know where he was getting his information from and what it was. I ended up just returning to my hotel and tried to read bits of the bible that seemed to leap off the page at me. Morning came and, after breakfast, I called the police saying I had been poisoned. The police came and talked to the hotel manager, whom I had known from cadets and the waitress who I knew from school, and decided the best thing to do would be to take me to the mental hospital, so off I went again.

Time in there passed slowly until I met a young woman who kind of had her act together. She was a bit older than me, had been a model and did well at it. We used to go into the visiting rooms and talk for hours. She wanted me to go with her to Jamaica where she had family but I was mostly just in the relationship to pass the time. I still had my heart set on fictional relationships that emanated from my delusional mind. That was such a terrible time for me, to be sent back to a place where I had already locked up twice before.

Awful as it may seem, I think it was what was best for me, because my mind was fabricating a running dialogue of strange instructions. For awhile, I believed there were cameras in my eyes and that some type of device could read my thoughts. The delusions would tell me each time a commercial came on TV that someone had just bought that product for me. Outlandish stuff and there was no way to make it go away but sit and wait, and sit and wait, be treated like a child and pace the hallways, constantly harassed for cigarettes.

For the first time in my life, I was feeling so horrible that I really wanted to kill myself. Again, the staff treated me horribly. I had done serious damage to my knees doing all that running in Vancouver and I could barely walk. I smoked, at the time, and was assigned a room at the end of a long hallway in the ward (10-1A again). Later, a nurse, feeling quite self-righteous, told me they had put me there so I would smoke less. I couldn't believe the cruelty.

I tried to tell them I was in severe pain and it felt like my knees were going to fall apart. After a lot of complaining, they sent me to see the medical doctor and he referred me to an orthopedic surgeon. The earliest appointment I could get was three months away. It was awful to have to wait but, at least, something was being done. Two months later, one of the nurses told me she had cancelled my appointment because she didn't think I needed it. It took me years to get enough stability in my life to see another doctor.

That, in itself, was heartbreaking but even worse was the day that, without even coming to see me, my dad dropped off a duffle bag with some clothes in it, and left instructions that I might as well go back to Vancouver when I was released. What really got me was that I had left a massive book collection, a good deal of furniture and comic, sports card and coin collections in his house. He had no intention to let me have any of it. Just to help make ends meet when I was on the coast, he had sold my three cars for $50 each when they only needed minor fixing and could have gotten me work.

The big difference about this hospital stay was that I was starting to realize that I couldn't run from my problems. I had to face them. I didn't accept this totally, but was starting to think about it. After a few weeks, I had a committal trial and my lawyer just sat and didn't say a thing. I got really pissed off at all this and called a legal hotline, explaining to the lawyer they connected me with that while I certainly did have problems, most of them were because my dad was an abusive alcoholic. Although this was only partially true, it was enough to get me released when I got around to having my next competency hearing.

Years later, my sister told me that they probably shouldn't have released me because I simply hadn't gotten better in any way. But I preferred my freedom to my sanity. That hospital had turned me into an animal and animals always choose to be free. I found an apartment but couldn't move in for two weeks so I moved in temporarily with the Jamaican girl.

Before I went to her place, she was extremely positive, talking about how she would make me pizza and we would stay up to watch CBC Late Night's old black-and-white movies. For the first few nights, she tried to seduce me but I wouldn't have any of it. It was nice to lie down together and cuddle but sex was something sacred to me. I made up excuses and eventually she turned into a total monster. She would scream and yell all kinds of insults and obscenities, and call her parents and yell at them.

On one occasion, she knew I had no money yet insisted I come along with her to a downtown restaurant, where she sat and ordered herself some food but wouldn't share. I got a small bit of satisfaction out of watching her throw up after that at the bus stop. I hated staying with her but really had nowhere else to go.

When I finally got my apartment, I cut all ties with the Jamaican girl and, years later, I heard she had killed herself. I felt sad about that and, in my mind, I had already forgiven her for the way she treated me. I would hear of a lot of deaths of people with mental illnesses, some from suicide, a lot from things like a poor diet, or cancer from all the cigarettes mentally ill people tend to smoke. Once I read a Danish study that found most people who try to kill themselves would die simply from lack of giving a shit within five years of their first attempt. I am grateful to sit here typing these words, knowing I made it past that grim line in the sand.

Through The Withering Storm

Living alone in that apartment wasn't too bad. I wasn't in the best part of town but I was close to Edmonton's scenic river valley so I could go for long bike rides and walks. I spent a lot of my money on junk food, everything from gelatin that I didn't really know how to make to about 50 pizzas over the course of three months. I even got some work in while I was there. I was hired as part of a crew that was doing a major shutdown at a chemical plant. When I was working, I would have to climb inside a reactor in a chemical protection suit and use long metal sticks we called fish tape to knock loose the encrusted catalyst out of hundreds of 40-foot pipes above our heads. The job was 12 hours a day and travel time was two hours each way. I only lasted about four or five days but that was enough to keep me in cigarettes and pizza for quite a while.

Just like the last time, I stopped taking my medication soon after leaving hospital and soon returned to the cycle of delusions and auditory hallucinations. It is so hard to describe a delusion. It's like a thought that forces its way into your mind without permission. I would turn on the radio and think the announcers were talking about me and could see and hear me. It was impossible to shut them out.

The three months I spent in that apartment weren't all horror and boredom. I had computer games, a bike, a TV and pigeons. On the ledge of a building, beside the one I lived in, there were always pigeons crapping on everything and making all kinds of racket all hours of the night and day. One day, it was particularly hot so I left a window open and in the morning when I woke up there was a pigeon in my kitchen. Outside, they seem harmless, but in an enclosed space these things can sure move a lot of wind. It took me nearly 10 minutes to chase the damn thing back out the window and then I had one heck of a mess to clean up.

Not long after that, I was going through my desk and I found a paper that my old friend Jason from Vancouver had written out for me. It was his sister's address and phone number and I remembered he had said if I ever needed anything to call him. I desperately wanted to get out of Edmonton again so I dialed the number. I don't know why we were such good friends. We were 10 years apart and he was from a wealthy family but we really did get along well. He encouraged me to come back out to the coast and said he could help find me a job and we could share an apartment. That was all the encouragement I needed.

It was only two weeks to the end of the month when I made the decision to head for Vancouver again and that meant I wouldn't get my damage deposit back, which in turn meant I wouldn't have much money to spare. But my mind was made up.

About a week before I left, a bunch of family and friends went to a bar where my brother was playing his guitar on stage and a friend of my brother's gave me some advice about medications and mental illness. The main thing, he said, was not to get too hung up inside your own head and to make sure you have a network of friends you can talk to. Sadly, this was enough for him but it wouldn't prove to be enough for me.

At the end of that month I bought my bus ticket and headed out once again, for disaster, adventure and more.

Through The Withering Storm

Chapter Eight: Trading Sanity for Freedom

It was a long bus ride heading across B.C. to Vancouver, more than 13 hours. I was never really bored because the scenery is incredible the whole way through, plus I often made friends with people on the bus and talked with them for the many hours it took to get to where we were going. Little did I know, that if I had booked ahead, taking a flight would be about the same cost and would only take an hour.

It was a bright and sunny day when I got to the bus terminal in Vancouver. My bags were stuffed with everything I could bring, even a small black and white TV. I grabbed a city bus over to the other side of the harbor to North Vancouver, over Lion's Gate Bridge. Seeing the mountains and the ocean all around gave me the feeling that summer was just beginning and a whole world of possibilities lay before me was just wonderful.

I got to the North Shore, took a cab to the house Jason was sharing and knocked on the door, not knowing what to expect. My old buddy greeted me with a cold beer and we sat on the back porch looking out at the ocean smoking cigarettes. It was as friendly a welcome that a guy could ever expect. Jason even let me take his motorbike for a spin.

I took his bike up a long, curvy mountain road and, on the way back down, the engine seized. A friendly motorist gave me some oil and I poured it in, hoping it would work. Luckily it did, but after I stopped at a gas station and went back up the mountainside to get to my friend's house, I stalled the bike and it fell over. I eventually got it back to the house, but was reluctant to ride it anymore, even though I had my motorcycle license.

We stayed at the house that night and the next day Jason sent me to the Hostelling International youth hostel which was a converted old army barracks right by the beach in Vancouver's west end. I booked us rooms and Jason went out looking for an apartment. We made a few calls and, the next day, even though I wanted to sleep in, he got me up and working, cleaning the hostel for which we were rewarded with a free night's stay. Then, I hit the sports fields and played baseball and soccer until my legs were burned so red they could have been hot wings.

The very next day, we found a place in North Vancouver, just a one bedroom for $600 a month but it was nice. It had a shag carpet, track lighting and lots of nice wooden trim, from the saloon-style doors to the paneling behind the lights. It was home. It didn't hurt that there was a fast food joint just half a block away either. The first night we didn't have any bedding with us so I ended up sleeping in the closet to try and keep warm. Jason rolled himself up in the shower curtain. Right away, with the help of my new roommate's sister, we got beds and a little furniture. I would have killed for a computer at that point but they were way too expensive back then.

I didn't have much money to spend and wasn't working, so I ended up reading a lot of great books that summer. I remember reading the *Caine Mutiny* and Stephen Coonts' book *Flight of the Intruder*. I really liked military books back then. I also read a lot of James Bond novels. Often, Jason and I would go out for breakfast and, if he had the day off, we would play tennis in the hot sun then, afterwards, eat ice cream. It was pretty idyllic for a

Through The Withering Storm

while, especially because I didn't have many delusions and even had nice dreams once in a while. Something about the sea air maybe or just being away from all the bad memories from school and the hospital.

Not long into that summer, I found an ad in an employment newspaper that said you could get government financing to learn how to fly. I had been fascinated with flying ever since I was 12 and first went up in a glider through Air Cadets. I called the number and asked for an introductory flight. The person on the phone said to come down and ask for Derek. When I got there, it turned out that Derek was one of my old cadet buddies from St. Albert. We went up and we did all kinds of turns and dives and had a whale of a time. I was hooked. The feeling of having a powerful engine propel you aloft and being able to move your hands and feet left and right to feel the wind rushing over your wings was absolutely incredible – much better than any sports car or fancy motorbike. This is what I wanted and I was determined to succeed. I booked an appointment with the main office, filled out the forms and patiently waited to see if I would get the student loan to fly for a living.

A long time back, Jason had seen me as a special project. He was much older than me, and once I read a letter his girlfriend had written him in which he told her he had taken pity on me and decided to help me out of the goodness of his heart. Although I would normally hope for something like this to happen, the tragic thing was that perhaps it was the worst thing for me at this time. Jason was no therapist and he certainly was no psychiatrist. His theory was that I was sick (and there were many times when he had seen me very mentally sick) and he could 'cure' me by being my friend. He did help me with housing and school but, after a while, he got tired of bailing me out and lending me money and then I was much worse off than before.

At one point, things were getting a bit out of hand so he said I had to get a job or move out by the end of the month. He couldn't really say that because both of our names were on the lease but I wanted a job anyway so out I went. I filled out quite a number of applications and ended up getting a job at a car wash, which was probably the worst job a person could get this side of telemarketing but it still had its benefits. One of them was a cute girl named Dianne who I think liked me, too. One night, she invited me to a party and I really wanted to go. It would have been a special night for us, I think, but I had come down with bronchitis and was sick as a dog. She sounded heartbroken when I called her.

All this time Jason had been keeping in touch with Sharon, the Australian girl we knew from the hostel downtown the year before and, a couple of weeks after I got that job, she came to visit us. The very first night she and Jason were sleeping together and I warned him that, because of that, it wouldn't last more than three months. "I can't believe how much I love her man!" he said to me.

When the end of that month came, I don't know why I was so irresponsible but I took the money I had for rent, and rented a car and drove to Seattle. It was one of the most fun things I had ever done. I felt so free once I got across the border. I tooled around Seattle in my little station wagon and had a grand old time. At one point, I stopped for gas and could hardly believe my eyes — there was beer everywhere. It was sold in gas stations. I didn't understand how they got people to refrain from drinking and driving. I bought

Through The Withering Storm

myself a case of 12 bottles (which was only about five bucks) and drove around drinking beer after beer.

I started to realize that I was going to have to pay a lot of money for all the kilometers on this car so I was going to do what a friend did when he put too many clicks on his mom's van. I would have to jack up the front and drive in reverse. I didn't know if it would work on this car so I started out driving around in reverse and, as I was circling in the parking lot backwards, I got thirsty, so I grabbed another beer. I wonder what a police officer would have done with me being underage, stunting, and drunk as a monkey. He would have locked me up for sure. But I got away with it, stupid as it was. I didn't get any kilometers off the wagon but it was kind of fun just the same.

After my little merry-go-round ride, I headed downtown, in dire need of a bathroom. I found a parking spot, carefully parallel parked the station wagon and went into an adjoining park to do my business. I was just undoing my fly when I heard a loud "Hey! Hey! What are you doing?"

"What does it look like I'm doing?" I replied.

"There's a bathroom in the hotel across the street!" came the answer back. I looked up and there was a whole row of lit-up windows, each with a person looking out at me while I was trying to water the shrubs. I was a little embarrassed but really too drunk to care.

As the morning rolled around I headed back for Vancouver and managed to get the car back after only having it for 24 hours. But I did put 700 km. on it so they charged me royally. I went back to the apartment and slept a long time.

A few days had passed, when one night I came home and my roommate was being a real jerk about the fact that Sharon had a headache. I could understand him wanting me to be quiet but the guy yelled at me just for stirring my tea. I made a comment about ridiculous mollycoddling and he came into my room, grabbed me by the throat, shook me and said I was going to learn some compassion. I could have killed him. As it was, I wanted to call the police and have him charged. But he was already one step ahead of me. He had picked up the phone in the other room and dialed a few random numbers so I couldn't call anyone. Then he came and said I had to get out right then and there. The only thing that kept me from doing something nasty was that he gave me $50 (I still hadn't paid any rent) and called ahead to the hostel in North Vancouver for me. So, now I had a job but was back to being semi-homeless.

That very week I got some good news in the mail. My student loan was approved and I could start learning to fly. This had to be the most amazing time of my life. Every day I flew, I was facing a new challenge. My lessons would include lessons on recovering from a spiral dive, nosing up until you fall out of the air and recovering, balancing the aircraft's rudder and ailerons to make a smooth and easy turn. And then there was landing.

When you land a plane, you have to judge from a long way back exactly when to cut power, when to start letting the plane lose altitude so you can glide in all the way without adding or subtracting power. After a while it gets easy but, when you are learning, it's like a mystical art. When I had spare time from flying, I tried to keep my nose buried in flight manuals and information my instructors gave me. For the first time in a long time, I really felt good about what I was doing.

In order to save money, I moved downtown where I could get a cheaper room and cheap meals at various soup kitchens. There was also a drop-in center where I could take computer classes, work out, play chess and use their library. It was at this time I ran into a man named Dean. I don't know how much of what he said was true but from what I understood he was some type of U.S. Marine, probably in the reserves. He had a thick American accent and talked big. One night, he and I went out on the town with one of his friends and he kept doing things like buzzing the information button at the train station and saying "How do I get from here to there?" He would also walk up to Asian people and make karate noises and wave his hands at them like he was going to strike. I should have seen him then for the goofball he was, but he had a lot of charisma and I was, at this point, short one best friend.

     I wasn't doing much at that time but waiting for my ground school classes to start. I had the weekend off and so Dean and I decided we were going to spend it in Seattle. We rode the Greyhound bus down and when we got to the border, just as we were lining up to go through, Dean turned to me and said, "Dude — I don't know you!" I didn't know how to take this but when I got up to the front of the line the customs agent gave me a real hassle. He asked me if I had ever been to the U.S. before. I stupidly told him the truth, that I was a student pilot and had been to the U.S. three times the day before. I think that got to him but, when I got pissed off and wouldn't let him search my bags, he turned me back. We ended up hitching rides, taking cabs and buses and after a long trip to nowhere we ended up back at the hostel.

     The next day we headed out for Seattle again, this time ready to take a little bullshit, and made it through. We checked in to a half-decent hotel and set out to explore the city. Dean had a gift with women.

He met a girl at a restaurant and ended up necking with her. He met another in the hotel and ended up sleeping with her. It was unbelievable.

One day, he decided he wanted to go fishing so he booked a trip for us down to a place called Centralia, Washington. Everything up to this point had been on my credit card, which was now maxed out. Dean kept making claims that his dad was wealthy and he would more than pay me back. The fishing tour was $300 for just one day, but again, I was reassured that it would all be repaid. The trip was fun; we got a couple of huge salmon and just missed by a week meeting Chuck Yeager, the famous pilot depicted in the movie *The Right Stuff*. He was a fan of the same fishing tour. For a couple of hours, having missed our bus, we went from restaurant to restaurant unsuccessfully trying to sell our fish and then ended up paying a teenager with a bad cheque to drive us back to Seattle.

The next day, from the hotel room, I was having a cool chat on the phone with Sharon, who was still in Vancouver, when Dean came into our hotel room with a panicked look on his face.

"Dude-put the phone down! Put the phone down!" he kept saying until I hung it up. "United States Customs and Immigration is downstairs right now with weapons drawn looking for us!" At that point I wanted to go and talk to them, not thinking they would arrest me since I had done nothing wrong. But Dean looked really worried.

I still hadn't seen through all his lies and bullshit so I decided to indulge him and stay hidden in my room for a short while, then went to Greyhound station to get us tickets out of town. When I tried to buy them the lady at the counter said that she recognized my name from somewhere, but by a stroke of luck she didn't report me to anyone. It is funny but it seems that a large portion of people in the US would rather help someone go free than turn them over to the authorities. At least, that was what I believe happened in my case.

When I got back to the room, Dean and I decided to take a walk to buy cigarettes, and on the way back a couple of guys yelled something at us and Dean went to challenge them. It turned out they were a couple of gay guys just coming out of a gay bar and one of them invited us to a party at his ranch. We agreed to go, ignoring all the signs that they were coming on to us, and down to Mount Rainer we drove. We spent the night there then got a lift into a nearby small town and got a motel room. Our plan was to head to Dean's hometown and then, if the heat wasn't off, we would join the Marine Corps where we couldn't be touched. I just liked the idea of getting a free helicopter license instead of paying more than $20,000 for my fixed-wing license. As long as I was flying, I figured things would be okay.

At one point in our journey, we found a U.S. Army recruiting station and went in to see if they took Canadians. They had me sit down, write a test and went over some of the things I could do in the Army. I scored in the 92nd percentile on the test, which was pretty good, and they were just about ready to induct me into the Army right there. Then, one of the guys in the office said he went to Canada a lot with a group he was affiliated with, and he started singing 'Oh Canada'. This really shook me up. Even brought a tear to my eye, from that point on I decided I wasn't going to serve any foreign power. I was much too much of a Canadian patriot.

We spent a couple more days bumming around from motel room to motel room and at some point I lost my credit card, probably to a clerk who had found out it was maxed. Dean and I ended up getting a ride with a series of truckers all the way to Los Angeles. When we crossed the border from Oregon into California, I could hardly believe I was so far from home, so far from my family and all by myself. I felt some pride but a lot of fear as well. I had no medical insurance and I was starting to have serious doubts about Dean and his loyalties. The bastard had been repeatedly lying and ripping off people all throughout our trip and I started to get a strong feeling he was ripping me off, too.

Within about an hour of being dropped off in L.A., we got a ride from three really cute California girls all the way to Dean's hometown of Hemet, Calif. We stopped at a corner store in the middle of town. I wanted to wait with the girls and Dean wanted to go to his friend's house. I told him to go there and come back and that was it. I never laid eyes on Dean again.

I had paid for and traveled with him all the way from Vancouver to Southern California. Without a word he just took off and left me sitting with no money, no passport, no credit cards, and no food. I even went to the police but they wouldn't help me.

Getting home was a long and tiring adventure. The first thing that happened, after the girls got tired of waiting and left, was that some guy came up to me, said he knew me, that I had been to his house. I didn't know this guy from Adam but wasn't about to contradict him. I just said, "Yeah, that's right. By the way, do you have that quarter you owe me?" A quarter wasn't much cash but I didn't figure this guy had much and I needed some candy or something to keep me going.

The next thing I did was go into Safeway and try to eat some free samples but was told I could just

Through The Withering Storm

have one. I ended up back at the corner store and because I hadn't had any sleep since Oregon, I sat down on a pop display and ended up nodding off. A cop, who told me to go outside and sleep, eventually woke me up.

I couldn't get over the whole attitude difference between American police and Canadian, especially in small towns. The American ones didn't seem to want to help at all, even though a crime had been committed. Canadian cops (probably for lack of anything better to do) would go way out of their way to help you.

I didn't really know what to do but the first order of business was food, so I went to another convenience store, explained that I was Canadian and had been ripped off and asked if I could do some sweeping or something for a bag of chips or a microwave burger. Every time I asked a convenience store clerk this I was rewarded with free food, without having to do any work. Once again, this was a testament to the Americans who defy the stereotypes of many people who never get to see the real America.

I caught a ride from there with a fellow who took me to another gas station further up the highway and I ended up sleeping in a ditch and getting a sun burn on half my face. I was so tired at that point I went into a pay toilet and fell asleep while people who probably really had to go were banging on the door. There were a bunch of Mexicans at that station trying to get rides as well and I will never know why but one of them gave me a pack of cigarettes when it didn't seem like any of them had anything to give. To add to that little kindness, when I got a ride, the lady behind the counter gave me five bucks.

After a couple of more rides and another day gone by, I met a man named David who saw me as a young kid in over his head and took me into his home, let me clean up, have a decent sleep and even offered to lend me the money to get home. I wouldn't take his money but he did give me a ride up to another truck stop where I would have an easier time of hitching home. One of the strange aspects about the time I spent with Dave, (with whom I still communicate once or twice a year) was that at one point he had to go into work so I stayed in the car and didn't even fall asleep completely. I had a real life hallucination that I was talking with an evil entity right there in front of me.

    The beast that had been tamed with sun baths, long sleeps and many hours of tennis and ice cream was starting to surface again. If I didn't get home, there would be no way in hell I could get treatment, having no traveler's insurance. I stayed in the truck stop Dave took me to for quite a while, borrowing and begging to eat and smoke. After what seemed like a couple of days but was likely closer to a week, I got a ride to yet another truck stop, this one on the road going north. It wasn't as busy as the others but was heading in the right direction. When I got to this one, there was a waiter there who fed me for free, let me stay over at his house, and when the time came, let me drive his car most of the way up California where I could get another ride. I just couldn't believe that someone could take in a stranger like that and literally save his life. I was deeply touched. I certainly hadn't seen much kindness like that back home, aside from Jason.

    When he announced it was time to give me a lift up north to a town called Redding, all he did was get in his car and fall asleep while I drove these incredible coastal highways. At first, I wanted to be responsible so I just did the speed limit but, at the ear-

Through The Withering Storm

splitting sound of an air horn, I looked in my mirror and saw a massive logging truck right on my bumper. That woke my friend up and he asked how fast I was driving. "Sixty-five, the speed limit." I said.

"Do ninety," he replied, and went back to sleep.

By this point in my strange adventure, my sister had sent me money, so all I had to do when we got to our destination was get on the bus. It was even a longer ride than the Edmonton-Vancouver route, but I made it through and when I got over the Canadian border I stopped for a moment, kneeled down and kissed the Canadian pavement. I was home.

After finally arriving in downtown Vancouver, I checked into a cheap hotel by the train station and had one of the best sleeps of my life. Then, I went down to the social services office and got some money for rent and food. I should have spent the money on those things but instead I decided to go buy a plane ticket to Edmonton. It was almost my birthday at that point and I wanted to spend it with my family.

My plane flew out the next day and I was lucky enough to meet a man on the flight who gave me a ride all the way into St. Albert. My parents invited me for supper but said I had to stay somewhere else. Everything about that old house reeked of bad memories and ongoing suffering. I had cried so many tears there, got drunk so many times and experienced all the bad and good a young man could handle. We had a sparse meal of canned ham and eggs, leaving me the impression that my folks were worse off than they let on. I then phoned up a cadet buddy and he said I could stay with him so I rode the bus out to his rented house in Edmonton.

I lived large while I was there, putting money down on a car I was to come back and pay for and then drive to Vancouver. I also ate out nearly every meal and went to the amusement park in West Edmonton Mall. While I was in Edmonton, I looked up and found a phone number for Laurie, the girl I met at summer camp back in 1987.

When I got back to Vancouver, I moved right back into my old apartment with Jason. Sharon had left him and headed home to Australia. When they first hooked up he said to me, "I can't believe how much I love her man." And now he was saying, "I can't believe she took the coffee maker."

On my 20th birthday, Dec. 2, 1991, I phoned Laurie and we had a long talk. I kind of wish I had never had strong feelings for her because she was such a nice person to have just as a friend. Not only was she pretty, kind and caring, she had one hell of a sense of humor. I called her again over the next few weeks a number of times and finally she asked me to stop calling.

I was starting to fall into the old seasonal illness again and was extremely confused about a lot of things. I started having delusions that Laurie wanted to marry me, that she wanted to help me get on my feet – literally. I hallucinated her saying that I could live with her until I got the surgery on my knees I so desperately wanted. I wrote her a long letter and let loose all of my feelings, real and not so real. Then, I walked to the corner store to get stamps to send the letter.

When I dropped it in the mailbox, I felt a dark and deep sensation that went from head to toe.

Chapter Nine: The Edge of Understanding and Beyond

I knew I was sick and that Laurie didn't love me. Deep down I knew this but the delusions were forcing me to do things that drove everyone away. I didn't know what to do at that point so I phoned the suicide hotline trying to get help, not really having a clue where to get it or even what kind of help I needed. I reached the suicide line but by some odd quirk of fate it was just a recorded message.

Over the next while, I sent a few letters and tried to call Laurie but neither method elicited any kind of response. I was really sick. I knew I couldn't go back to flying and certainly didn't want to go in the hospital again. The last month of the lease on our apartment came and went so I moved to the hostel near the waterfront in North Vancouver again and parted company with Jason.

I started to get much worse, yelling things to myself while I was alone in my room, hanging out at a pub thinking people were trying to tell me I owned the place. It's embarrassing and painful to think back on that time but, at least, I have now become sane enough to know when I need help and where to get it.

One day I woke up, walked out of the hostel and went for quite a long walk. I had a delusion that I had been asleep for hundreds of years and that I was living in a reconstructed Vancouver on the moon. One side of my brain was fighting the other for control. My sane side wanted me to keep walking and jump off the middle of the Lion's Gate Bridge. I got halfway there and called the police thinking I had been given LSD or another hallucinogenic drug. A really huge police officer came and escorted me to the

Lion's Gate Hospital, where I was to spend the next few weeks. It was a nice place to be, actually. The food was really good and the staff was kind and caring.

During the six weeks or so I was there, I met a pretty and sweet young woman, whose name escapes me, who seemed to really like me. After being dumped so many times, I didn't understand why anyone would like me but she did. It is quite possible that she was acting under delusions as I was, because one day she looked at me and said, "I have something to give you." and she put a silver chain around my neck and bent down right to the floor like I was something to be worshipped. I guided her up to the standing position again, gave her a little kiss and thanked her. She was lovely but the poor girl was always so sad for some reason. I never saw her again after I left.

I made a decision at that point that I was going to take my medications and follow the doctor's advice no matter how hard it got to be. I thought if I could do this I would get Laurie back, even though she never really was mine. When I got out of hospital, I took the last of my money and bought a bus ticket back to Edmonton, hoping to get into a hospital there. The ride was long and painful. When I had left Lion's Gate, they had given me a time-release injection that wasn't even the right medication for a person with bipolar disorder. I was so discombobulated that I kept taking acetaminophen and trying to sleep through the arduous 13-hour journey.

When I finally got to Edmonton, I didn't have much luck. All the hospitals were full so I ended up living in a homeless shelter and being harassed for money and cigarettes again, this time in even worse shape to be able to deal with such things. I was also

Through The Withering Storm

eating pretty bad food and living with sanitary conditions much below what I had been used to. In Vancouver, it rains all winter mostly and when the rain stops it gives off a fresh and clean sort of smell. In Edmonton, it snows all winter and thousands of tons of sand are spread on the roads, which makes the whole place take on a dusty and dingy air.

Eventually, a room opened up in a hospital and with the urging of my dad, I was admitted to the University Hospital, probably the best place in the region to be if you're sick. Within a couple of days of getting into the hospital as a psychiatric patient, I was given the news that my aunt had died of a drug overdose. She suffered from depression and I hadn't seen her in years, though at one time she had spent a lot of time with our family and I had thought she was a fairly good person.

I spent the next while in a deep depression, sad for my aunt; sad for all the friends I left behind on the coast. I was also feeling my life was over now that I could no longer fly and I would have a hard time working or earning a living at all. One of the worst things about being the hospital was that I had no money left and no cigarettes. I ended up taking butts out of ashtrays and smoking them in my pipe, a rank and vile-smelling substitute for smoking.

One day my dad came in and one of the nurses got really mad at him for neglecting my needs. As a result, he brought some cigarettes that had belonged to my deceased aunt Joanne. My life seemed pretty bleak but it is amazing how the mind and body can adapt to terrible situations. Within a couple of months, I was out and in a couple more I had registered to go back to school. I also managed to quit drinking and ran into a good friend who lived just a block away. We would often get together to play cards, go to church and shoot pool. Money was so tight then I used to just barely scrape by, using my bike instead of the bus and skimping on things like proper food just to have a dollar to play pool. For a while, I had a job as a security guard but I was in no shape yet to hold down a responsible job like that.

It seemed to take forever but school eventually started and I made some friends including a very special friend named Debbie who became my very first girlfriend. I still hang out with Debbie. We have been close since that very first day we met on the front steps of our school and I took her to breakfast across the street.

My trip to the U of A hospital did not prove to be my last, despite my resolution to take my medications and accept treatment. When I went back to school, I found that one of the drugs I was on, lithium, left my hands shaking like an old man and I couldn't write legibly so I went off of it. This was to prove a horrible mistake. After another period of delusions and tattered friendships, I was again forcibly taken to the hospital and another month of my life was wasted, spent pacing hallways and denying treatment and having run-ins with hospital staff and patients.

On and on, this cycle went over the years. I couldn't understand why no matter what I did or how hard I worked, or how well I seemed to do I would end up ranting and raving in a psych ward or the provincial mental hospital. A turning point came when I went to my doctor and practically begged him to put me on something different than Tegratol (which left me so restless and edgy I couldn't function) or Lithium. He decided to try me out on something relatively new and yet to be proven drug called Depekane. This drug changed my life, all of a sudden I could think more clearly and function without the

Through The Withering Storm

highs and lows, and for years it kept me on an even keel and out of the hospital except for an admission for depression, which was far better than being admitted forcibly for delusions.

This new medication helped so much that I went on to get jobs and a car and I had many good times with Debbie, though now just a friend and no longer a lover. It was so good that I nearly forgot I had a mental illness. Unfortunately, I was wrong. After a couple of years of doing well, I found that I was feeling drugged and unable to carry out my daily tasks, so I thought that if I halved my Depekane, I would be fine. I was, for a while. But, after about a year or so, I was smack dab in the middle of the worst condition I had ever been in. My neighbors who had become close friends were watching me deteriorate, wasting away from 200 to 150 pounds, getting all kinds of strange ideas in my head, everything from the classic "I think for some reason I own this building" to the other main delusion of people with my problem "I'm secretly royalty." I had even found out that I could write letters to the Prime Minister and the Governor General on the Internet and I wrote them asking for a disability increase and was certain it was just days until they would do so.

It would have been better if things had stopped at that point but, with my delusions, came a need for money and I applied for credit and somehow got it. By the time my family and the clinic I went to had intervened to the point where I could be taken to the hospital, I was walking around with $15,000 worth of credit cards in my pocket and nothing but an $800 a month disability cheque coming in. Again, I wish this had been the worst of my problems but, again, it wasn't.

LEIF GREGERSEN

I was about to spend the longest and most painful hospital visit I have had to endure in my life. For the next six months, I went through beatings (from staff and patients), treatments with improper medications, denial of any contact with the outside world and denial of any of my needs. I spent at least 100 days locked in a room with a window to see in from the outside, a mattress and a blanket and absolutely nothing else. I used to get so angry, I would rant and rave inside that room, kick the door, scream, do anything I possibly could to make myself heard. It was unbelievable torture and none of the staff needed a reason to put me in there. I know one of them used to put me in the solitary room for fun. Not all the staff were bad, but I am quite sure now that at least two or three of them were borderline psychopathic.

I can remember now in the worst part of that experience saying to myself that this would end, this will pass, this will all one day be over. Although I still wake up sometimes with screaming and kicking nightmares from that experience, it did end and life for me has begun again.

It is so hard when you are in an institution like that to adjust to being in there, but it is even harder to get out. The recidivism rate of Alberta Hospital is probably close to 100 per cent but here I am, nearly 10 years and counting. When I got out, I took things one small step at a time. I started out sleeping most of the day and just reading a little or taking a short bus ride, then working my way up to my addictions meetings. Small step by small step, over a course of years, I once again found a job, saved up for a car and now I live just about totally independent in my own apartment, working out three or four times a week and writing as much as I can. Writing not to complain to the world what has happened to me but writing to show the world that those people you see begging change or dressed funny or walking down the street talking to themselves are our mothers, brothers, sisters, cousins. People that need help, need kindness and understanding, people that have value in this society, not people to be shunned and insulted.

It was an especially difficult journey but I like to think I have done well for myself, not just as a mentally ill person, as a person period. What I was really searching for all that time was some kind of connection, some way out of the hell of isolation, the illness called bipolar disorder that causes so many people so much suffering; destroying friendships and families, causing depressions and suicides as well as so much misunderstanding and embarrassment.

I found that connection in Debbie. And I found it in my own family after many years of growing up, the critical discovery that I was not alone and didn't have to be isolated in my personal hell. Debbie may never be the partner I hoped at some times she could be, but she is someone who I care deeply for and cares deeply for me. When I have friends who tell me they were married 15 years or that they have had hundreds of girlfriends, people are always amazed that I still talk to my very first girlfriend every day.

It was different with Debbie though. She was such a caring person that I found I could be totally honest with her and, when I was, she let on to me that she had an uncle with the same problem. Many times people have asked why I am a certain way or why do I get a disability pension, and much more often than not when I tell them the truth, they tell me they have a friend or a family member who also suffers. Many times, they even tell me they themselves are sufferers. There are so many out there like me, like my departed aunt Joanne and my departed mother, Beverly Anne Gregersen. Maybe, if a few of us were not so alone and shunned, we could prevent some horrible losses from happening and all feel more like human beings.

Today, I think a lot of the nature of mental illness and how it impacts those around us. Often, I think a lot about how horribly ashamed and embarrassed I have been at different points of my life because of my illness and the things I have done under its far-reaching grip.

Many years have passed now since I gave up my wandering lifestyle and accepted the fact that I am a person with an illness that has to be treated, otherwise it will destroy me. I still feel the brunt of the shame and regret from a lot of the things I did while I was sick and, of course, it is a daily occurrence for me to run head-on into prejudices against those who are like me.

Despite the fact that I accepted my illness, I have been in hospitals to be treated for depression and mania many times. Seven years ago, however, I started to see a doctor with whom I could really talk, who was very intelligent and kind. I have stayed out of incarceration for this whole time and have started to build a decent life for myself. I now work as a security guard for movie sets and as a stagehand for concerts, making better money than I ever have. Although I spent five years in a group home, I now have my own place where I have time to write and read. And, most importantly, I have my freedom. I have even worked flying back into my life, going up every now and then just for a bit of fun, even though I will never earn a license.

Through The Withering Storm

My main enemy these days is no longer my illness, it is the stigma that remains about bipolar affective disorder. I have lost a lot of friends because of this stigma but have persevered. There is hope, especially now that I have written this book, that I can do just as much and be just as happy as anyone, so long as I keep working with my doctors and keep being honest instead of being afraid to reveal what is happening for fear I will be locked up for the rest of my life.

One in five people in North America will have to seek treatment at one point in their lives for a mental disorder but not all of them have to suffer. Understanding and education are the weapons in my daily war and there is no end of battles left to fight.

We had to take apart our souls
Our bodies, minds and brains
Filter it through with work and effort
And write out what then remains

You see when life kicks you in the head
And all but pain is gone
You become some kind of artist
And in that find a way to keep on keeping on

– Poem excerpt from *A Disadvantaged Shell* by Leif Gregersen

Made in the USA
Charleston, SC
12 November 2012